The

Frugal
Gambler

Second Edition

Other Books by Jean Scott

More Frugal Gambling

Tax Help for the Frugal Gambler
with Marissa Chien

The
Frugal Gambler

Jean Scott

Second Edition

HUNTINGTON PRESS
Las Vegas, Nevada

The Frugal Gambler—Second Edition

Published by
Huntington Press
3687 South Procyon Avenue
Las Vegas, Nevada 89103
(702) 252-0655 Phone
(702) 252-0675 Fax
e-mail: books@huntingtonpress.com

Previous editions copyrighted in
1998, 2000, 2001, 2002, 2003, 2004

ISBN 0-929712-42-0

Cover Photos: Jason Cox
Cover Design: Jason Cox and Bethany Coffey
Production: Jason Cox, Laurie Shaw
Illustrations & Interior Design: Bethany Coffey

To my beloved grandchildren, Kaitlynn and Zachary.
I love the way you have changed my life.

Acknowledgments

Thank you, Suzanne, for giving me the push to restart my inner writing machine, which had been silent for 20 years.

Thank you, Lenny, Max, Stanford, Dan, Jeff, and Bob. Not only were your books valuable guides, but your personal encouragement gave me added inspiration.

Thank you, fellow players, who have shared your computer "secrets" *and* become my friends — especially Marilyn and Dom.

Thank you, Angela, for taking my taped thoughts and putting them through your word processor, saving so much time for your computer-challenged mother who steadfastly refuses to come off the country backroads and get on the information superhighway.

An extra thanks to you, Deke Castleman, editor par excellence. You performed a miracle — taking my waterfall gush of jumbled thoughts and harnessing it into a smooth-flowing river contained neatly in its banks.

And a special thanks to you, Anthony Curtis. Once

upon a time, many years ago, we were both struggling citizens in the realm of Ku Pon. We traded ideas and shared dreams. Your publishing business grew big and your *Las Vegas Advisor* crowned me the Queen of Ku Pon. I knew all along you were good. Now your words are the authority on this land. I designate you our Prime Minister.

I will not thank you, Brad; that is too mild a word to convey what I feel about your love. We've lived this book together. I am only the designated scribe.

Contents

Foreword
by Anthony Curtis

In 1978, Ian Andersen wrote the classic (and classically titled) book, *Turning the Tables on Las Vegas*. In it, he outlined a strategy for combining a beatable game (blackjack) with an approach designed to exploit inherent weaknesses in the casino system to make money gambling. Though the science of profitable gambling was already known, Andersen elevated it to an art form.

I recall my exhilaration when I first read Andersen's masterpiece. Here was a practical model — a roadmap, if you will — that I could easily follow to beat the casinos at their own game. What a gas!

Nearly two decades later, as I read the manuscript for *The Frugal Gambler*, my thoughts flashed back to *Turning the Tables*. What I held in my hands was a new roadmap, eminently followable, that offered a plan tailored to the unique opportunities available now — opportunities created by cutthroat competition and prolific expansion in the casino world. Simply stated, Jean Scott has taken the beatable game of video poker, linked it to new loopholes, and given us a practical plan for turning today's casino system inside out.

Another day another way, though. Jean Scott's methods aren't as much about winning money as they are about getting the extra things that gambling brings: free rooms, free meals, free parties—even free airfare. That's where the "frugal" part comes in. If Jean Scott is anything at all, she's risk averse ("totally cheap" in layman's terms). Consequently, most of the techniques she shares in this book are within your financial means—you can count on it. As she likes to remind us, her favorite word is "free."

Do Jean's tactics work? Absolutely. For years I've marveled at her moves. I've watched her demolish the casinos with weapons of their own making—slot clubs, the comp system, funbooks, drawings, casino promotions, video poker, and anything else that was remotely vulnerable. Many of her exploits have been chronicled in the *Las Vegas Advisor*, where she was dubbed the "Queen of Ku Pon": staying free in Las Vegas for months at a time, finding profitable plays in the new breed of games like the Piggy Bankin' slot machines, and of course, doing us all proud by winning a new car in front of a nationwide audience on "48 Hours."

Successful professional gamblers describe the techniques they use to beat the casinos as "advantage play." Until now, the term has had meaning to only a select few within a close-knit fraternity. No longer. With *The Frugal Gambler*, Jean Scott brings advantage play to the masses.

Author's Note
to the Second Edition

I penned most of the words of the original *The Frugal Gambler* in 1996. To state it more accurately: I talked the information into a tape recorder; my daughter Angela transcribed it into her computer and printed it out; and I then took my blue pen to the hard copy for multiple revisions. I hadn't as yet jumped on the computer bandwagon.

My husband Brad and I had already spent 12 years visiting casinos, first as skilled weekend/vacation blackjack card counters, then as retired stay-as-long-as-we-could-get-free-rooms-and-food video poker players. For several years, I'd been urged by other players to share our secrets on how we could live such a fun and luxurious life with no outlay of our own money — though they wanted an impossible 25-words-or-less "silver bullet."

Okay, I figured I'd give them what they wanted — a gambling primer. It didn't turn out that way.

I quickly realized it would end up taking a whole book. Darn! I'd retired from teaching high school English, but here I was at work again, still teaching, but in a much different field. So I decided I'd make this the most complete gambling book any novice casino visitor would ever need. Then I could go back into retirement as simply another gambler who loved to play video poker.

Somehow my well-laid plans went astray, due mostly to a big weakness in my personality—I could never overcome my constant striving for perfection. By the time *The Frugal Gambler* was published in early 1998, I already had a foot-high pile of notes of things I "forgot" to put in the book. Aiding and abetting this never-ending search for perfection—or at least completeness—was the fact that casinos were constantly changing their programs and policies. I just had to help people adapt their play with constantly updated information.

It didn't help that Brad and I had done so well playing video poker at the quarter level that we'd moved up to playing higher stakes. Now we were learning how to deal with hosts, a comp system much more complex than slot-club benefits from the booth and mailed offers from marketing.

In addition to this, we sold our home in Indianapolis and became Las Vegas locals, giving us still another new perspective on casino play.

Six years of gathering new information culminated in a book 50% bigger than this one, supposedly the last word on the subject of casino gambling! *More Frugal Gambling* came out in November 2003. *Tax Help for the Frugal Gambler* followed quickly in January 2004.

Could I now retire—pleeeeeeeeez?

Enter my dearly beloved publisher, Anthony Curtis, and editor, Deke Castleman, at Huntington Press. Had I read *Frugal* 1 recently? Well, no. After all, I'd been very busy writing *Frugal* 2, and then enjoying its enthusiastic acceptance by the growing numbers of frugal fans. Anthony and Deke suggested I read it over and update some of the information before they sent it to the printers for a seventh reprinting.

Talk about spoiling someone's vacation!

Still, I sat down and read *The Frugal Gambler* from first page to last. It still covered the basics of casino gambling very well and there's still a need for a cornerstone book such as this. But I felt like the mother who'd had a second baby and momentarily forgot to give her first-born equal attention. It's now spring 2005 and there've been many changes in the casino world since 1996. So this is not a simple reprinting with a few details changed; this is a whole new edition.

I've kept all the fundamental information that for years made the first edition so valuable to players, but I've added some new material and updated a number of details, so you'll be better prepared to enter any 21st-century casino and know how to make your gambling dollar—and thus your entertainment time—last longer.

Introduction
From Uncle Wiggley to Deuces Wild

Playing games has always been in my blood. One of my earliest memories is sitting cross-legged on the floor playing Uncle Wiggley. I was three or four years old, still an only child. I'd pester my mother, "Please play a game with me." She was often at the ironing board or sewing machine and too busy to participate, but she'd say, "OK, honey, I'll play. You set it up."

I'd pull out the Uncle Wiggley board and twirl the spinner and take my turn—hop hop hop—moving the number of spaces the spinner indicated. Then I'd say, "It's your turn, Mother," and she'd say, "You spin for me." So I'd spin for her and move her game piece. Even though I was doing all the work, it didn't matter; I was playing a game and I was happy.

To this day I remember the intense feeling of competitiveness I had as a child. Even at age four and five, sitting at a Chutes and Ladders board, I played to win. It was a very important, even passionate, part of my life.

It may seem like a long way from a kiddy board game on a threadbare rug in a simple Pennsylvania home to dollar Deuces Wild and the luxurious hotel rooms, free meals, and first-class entertainment given to us by palace-like casinos all over the world. Yet the spirit is exactly the same — intense, competitive, playing to win.

Growing Up as a "PK"

Where I am today is even more remarkable considering where I was back then. My father is an evangelical fundamentalist minister, so I was a "PK," a preacher's kid. We had no cards or dice in our home. If a game that we wanted to play came with dice, we'd have to throw them away and use a spinner from one of our other kiddie games instead. Cards and dice were symbols of gambling, which was very much against our religion. But our family always played games. From the simple don't-have-to-read-the-rules games, I graduated to Chinese checkers, chess, and finally Monopoly, the ultimate of all board games, I thought.

Many first-born children are resentful of their younger siblings, but not I! I was exceedingly grateful when my parents provided me with two sisters with whom to play games. My parents were grateful too, because now I didn't pester them to play with me all the time. My family played games almost every night except Wednesdays (which was prayer-meeting night); on Sundays we played religious games. My mother would cook up a big bowl of popcorn and we'd pull out a board game. When we three girls were old enough to play Scrabble, the family's competitiveness really blossomed. My father is 90, and until a couple of years ago when his health failed one of his greatest pleasures in life was to get together with his three girls, play Scrabble, and beat all three of us. Even though he oversaw a very strict and religious household, the gaming spirit was strong.

Because we were not allowed to have playing cards in the house, I didn't learn the four suits until I was in my early thirties. We weren't even allowed to play games like Old Maid, because that would have had the appearance of sinful behavior. Someone might have seen us playing and thought we were engaged in a poker game! When I got married, I finally started to play cards, but not "real" card games. We went through a period of Old Maid, Rook, and Pit, just enough to broaden my life a little bit.

Gin Rummy Fun

When I was thirty-five, things changed: I left the fundamentalist environment and embarked on a new kind of life. That's when I finally decided it was okay to play games like gin rummy and poker, so I had to learn the suits. Even today, sometimes I still think of a club as a "clover" or a spade as a "digger," because that's the way I learned them. At that time I had a close friend who played a lot of cards. He taught me how to play gin rummy. I took to it immediately. We played for a penny a point and for years we kept a running total in a notebook; since he'd been playing all his life, I wound up owing him quite a lot of pennies. Luckily, he became my second husband so I never had to pay off! But this was my first experience playing a game for money, not just for the pleasurable feeling of competition and trying to win. Even though it was only pennies (that would never be paid), suddenly I realized that playing for real money added a whole new spice to the gaming experience that I had never known before.

Next came Tonk and Euchre, card games that are extremely popular in the Midwest. Both are played for money and my husband and I played them around the kitchen table with our friends, again just for small stakes. Then I started driving 30 miles to where my husband worked so I could play Tonk with him and his co-workers on their lunch hour. They played for dollars, and that's when my competitive spirit finally roared up from deep inside me like a geyser. I took to the higher stakes very quickly. I became an excellent Tonk player and found myself beating others who'd played a lot longer than I had. It was only then, several decades after Uncle Wiggley, that I realized I was a natural at gambling.

Eventually, my husband and I joined a Moose Lodge where there was a Tonk game from ten in the morning till midnight almost every day of the week. Whenever I had a spare hour or two from raising my children or teaching high school English, that's where I would be. The stakes were quite a bit higher; therefore, the challenge and pleasure were greater.

Neon Lights and Black Chips

I took my first trip to Las Vegas in 1984. Although I'd been playing cards for only a few years, my husband Brad had been gambling since he was five (he had two older brothers as teachers). But neither of us knew a thing about casino gambling, so we played the no-brainer slot machines and a little seat-of-the-pants low-stakes blackjack. We lost our entire gambling bankroll, but we enjoyed that trip so much that we knew we would return to Vegas as often as we could.

Hoping to improve our results, we attended a blackjack seminar in our hometown and learned basic strategy. Then we went to the library and put ourselves through a crash course on card counting. We practiced and practiced and practiced — and got good enough to raise the stakes considerably.

It's funny to think of it now, but we began our casino careers as high rollers. We bet green ($25) and black ($100) chips, and went on junkets to Las Vegas, Reno-Tahoe, and Atlantic City, sometimes on private casino airplanes. We ate in all the gourmet restaurants, saw the best shows, and had the most luxurious rooms. We were living the good life. Then we broadened our horizons and went on junkets to San Juan, Santo Domingo, even Monaco. That was the ultimate junket. Our airfare was paid, we stopped in Paris for four days, and then it was on to Monte Carlo, where everything was comped, even at the exorbitant European prices.

Looking back on that era, I feel we did fairly well for ourselves. We lost more money than we won, because we weren't the greatest card counters, but we made more than enough in comps to cover our losses. It was pretty heady living in the rarefied air of the high-roller.

Then in 1989, Brad retired and we decided that we wanted to spend more of our time in casino locations. That's when we started to consider a different lifestyle. We began to think that the way we were doing it — taking $3,000-$4,000 and flying to Tahoe for three or four days — was too hectic. Those few days just weren't long enough: we gambled too long, we didn't get enough sleep, and we didn't have enough time to enjoy all the "real-life" things that beckoned to us from outside the casino. Also, on occasion we'd lose a good portion of our gambling bankroll, and it all seemed too fleeting, too transitory, for the price we were paying.

So we decided to take the $3,000 or $4,000 and try to make it last longer — a lot longer — three or four weeks instead of three or four days. We knew that the best place to do it was Las Vegas, with its proliferation of competing casinos. We decided to trade the first-class short-term treatment for less luxurious amenities over a longer period of time and, in the process, reduce our gambling risk. Besides, about that time the casinos were starting to cut down considerably on what they were giving back in comps to table players; you had to bet more and more to get the good stuff. So we reduced our bets to red chips ($5) and spent a couple of years doing quite well working the lower end of the scale.

We now went to Las Vegas for a week, two weeks, three weeks at a time. We weren't staying at the higher-class hotels like Caesars Palace, but at older casinos like the Riviera, Holiday Inn (now Harrah's), and the Westward Ho. We learned how to work the comp system and discovered that we didn't miss the gourmet meals (even when it's free, fancy food isn't good for the waistline or the cholesterol count). Playing $5 and $10 blackjack, we could still get comps for all the food we could eat—at good buffets and coffee shops. We could also get our rooms at the discounted "casino rate" (typically 40%-50% off the rack rate). Occasionally, our combined blackjack action would earn us a free night or two.

Low-Roller Paradise Found

As time went by, I began to notice that Brad would be gone from the blackjack tables (while we were playing and being rated) for longer and longer periods. I wondered where he went, afraid the pit bosses would get after him for staying away from the table—just leaving his chips and disappearing. We already knew that you should leave the table as often as possible, because you were being rated by the hour and as long as you left your chips at the game, the comp clock kept ticking. Finally, he confessed that he was running over to the machines and playing video poker.

I thought, "Oh no, *not* video poker!" Everyone knows slot machine players are uninformed and can't win. I figured only a real loser would go from blackjack to video poker. Brad, on the other hand, looked at things differently. "But, Jean, I'm only putting in quarters and I'm not losing that much," he insisted. "Besides, it's so relaxing and fun."

And he was right. Blackjack gets tiring, particularly when you're counting cards. We couldn't play for long periods at a time, so following Brad's lead, I decided to take a (skeptical) look. When we left the tables and stopped the comp clock, I'd sit at the video poker machines, watching while he tried his luck.

Then in January 1990 we were playing at the Stardust when I noticed advertisements about a "slot club." When I investigated, I found that it didn't cost anything to join and members got comps, prizes, even cashback, for their play. I said to Brad, "As long as you're gonna be putting money into these machines, we might as well get something back for it."

I started reading articles in various gambling magazines which claimed that video poker was a game of skill and that the payback could be very good, almost 100%. We also found that at the end of our trips, the Stardust would give us back $40-$50, based solely on Brad's video poker play. Better yet, when we went home, we started getting mail from the Stardust—invitations for free nights and meals and parties—which reminded us of when we were high rollers.

The next time we went to Las Vegas, we took advantage of the free nights at the Stardust and we started joining every slot club we could. Brad and I use different surnames, so we opened up two separate accounts at each casino, and I started playing video poker, too. Also, we studied up on the optimal strategy for 9/6 Jacks or Better video poker, so although we weren't winning, we weren't losing much while the comps continued to roll in.

We started to get lots of our nights comped, and since we were retired and had all the time in the world, we didn't mind moving around a bit to take advantage of as many offers as we could at the different casinos where we were slot club VIPs. A casino would send me an offer in the mail for three free nights, and Brad would get the same offer on the same day in the same mailbox. By combining our six nights at casino A, then accepting an offer for four nights between us at casino B, as well as another four nights at casino C, we all of a sudden were staying in Las Vegas for 14 nights, without paying for a single one! In addition to this, any time we asked, we got our food comped.

The Joy of Video Poker

To top it all off, we discovered that video poker was far more enjoyable than blackjack. Playing 21 is hard. Card counting requires constant mental calculations. First you have to calculate the true count, then divide by the number of decks remaining to derive the running count, then figure out how much to bet. All the while you worry that the pit boss is on to you as a counter and — horror of horrors! — you'll get thrown out of the casino and have to start all over again somewhere else. I'd already been barred from one casino in Tahoe for counting cards, so these fears were genuine. And for me, there was a more pressing problem. I'd always played a good game of blackjack with basic strategy, but when I counted cards, I think my lips moved slightly. I was an English teacher and math never came easily to me, so when I counted, I had to do it almost verbally. It was exhausting!

But playing video poker, we could sit side by side at the machines and laugh and drink diet soda and not worry about a thing. We knew the Jacks or Better strategy so well that we barely had to think about it, and we were getting more comps than we did playing $5 and $10 blackjack. It was all so much more fun.

Before long, we started noticing Deuces Wild video poker machines and began talking to people who were playing them. We quickly learned that unlike Jacks or Better, the Deuces Wild variation was a positive game (meaning it paid back more than 100%). We went to Gamblers Book Club, paid $9.95 for a booklet on video poker in Las Vegas (by Lenny Frome), and studied the strategy for Deuces.

The first time we sat down in front of a Deuces Wild machine was New Year's Eve 1991. I held the book while Brad played, and every time a hand popped up that we weren't sure how to play, I looked it up on the chart. After a couple of hours of playing, I had a headache from all the smoke and noise and retired to the room, leaving the strategy book with Brad. About an hour later the phone rang. It was Brad. "Guess what? I just hit the $1,000 royal flush!" I laughed, "Well, I guess that pays for our $9.95 strategy book!"

The Queen of Comps

Soon it was smooth sailing. The comps kept rolling in, we learned to take advantage of promotions, we perfected the strategies for many of the video poker variations, and we were having a blast. We'd gone from $100 bets to $5 bets at blackjack, then to $1.25 a hand at video poker. We were getting more comps and freebies from the casinos playing $1.25 video poker than we ever did playing $25 blackjack. Our transition from high rollers to low rollers was complete.

For us, making the most of the low-roller system (initially) culminated in December-January 1993. During those two months we played no blackjack at all (except during special promotions). Instead, we sat at the video poker machines. This was the longest Las Vegas trip we had undertaken. We stayed for 50 days, including Christmas, New Years, and the Super Bowl. We paid for a room on only one night. (We could've gotten that night free too, but we didn't want to bother switching hotel rooms for a single night.) The only meals we paid for were those we ate outside of the hotel-casinos when we just couldn't face another free buffet or coffee shop (poor us!). And because we managed to hit five royal flush jackpots, at the end of those 50 days we went home with $1,500 more than we left with.

It was for those feats that the *Las Vegas Advisor*, the famous consumer's newsletter for Las Vegas visitors, pegged me the "'Queen of Ku Pon,' the ruling monarch of the mythical magical kingdom of Low Roller." And two years later, when CBS's news magazine "48 Hours" did an entire show on gambling, two segments were devoted to Brad and me and our money-saving exploits. While introducing our story, Dan Rather gave me the title that has stuck: the "Queen of Comps."

1

Raining on the Casino's Parade

We now make our home in Las Vegas, but for 17 years we traveled from Indiana and stayed free in casino hotels for increasingly higher numbers of nights. The year before we bought our Vegas condo, we stayed 191 nights free, compliments of a casino somewhere in the country, including all the food we could eat. So I'll be the first to admit that I'm a little obsessive about free rooms and comped meals, and I go to great lengths not to have to pay for what I can just as easily get gratis. It's probably true that not just anyone can be the Queen (or King) of Comps. But it's also true that even the most casual once-a-year casino visitor can profit from the hundreds of tips and hints in the following pages and learn to parlay the benefits of positive-expectation games, comps, promotions, slot club memberships, airline bumps, and miscellaneous tricks into a whole lot of free stuff along the way.

In fact, I'll begin by saying that the less you know about how casinos operate the better. How can that be? Because then I don't have to set you straight on the many untruths that people believe — and that the casinos use to their advantage — about how the whole gambling game is played. Let's take a look at a few of these myths.

Myth One
The casino will always make a big effort to get your business.

Well, you'd think this would be true, but I find it to be one of the most widespread untruths in the gambling business. Casinos don't do nearly as much as they could to get your business. They seem to feel that it's a kind of reverse *Field of Dreams* scenario: if *they* build it, *you* will come. And when they do try, the efforts more often than not are insufficient. Sometimes they run promotions and the casino employees aren't even aware of them!

My biggest gripe is with the way some casinos run their coupon programs. I don't know how many times I've sat down at a blackjack table, put down a coupon with my bet, and watched the dealer stop the game dead, pick up the coupon, read it with a puzzled expression on his face, and comment, "I've never seen one of these before. Must be some new program they came up with upstairs." Then the pit boss has to be called over, and invariably the same routine is repeated. By the time they've figured out how the coupon works, the whole table is mad at me for holding up the game.

Worse yet is when I sit down with a coupon and the dealer gives me a disparaging look or makes a sarcastic comment. The casino has paid a lot of money to have its coupons printed, promoted, and distributed so that more people will visit, and all the efforts are effectively negated by rude employees.

Another wasted opportunity is when a casino has a slot club, but you can't tell that it does. There's nothing on the machines that tells you that they're hooked up to a slot club. The slot club booth is hidden in an out-of-the-way corner someplace and there are no brochures or signs that tell you there's a slot club to join and freebies to acquire. Some casinos do a good job at promoting their slot clubs and promotions, but many don't. You have to hunt for what you want to find.

Myth Two
*The casino wants your name
and address for devious purposes.*

No, the casino wants your name and address so it can give you stuff. Unless you're cheating, are a fledgling card counter (and haven't figured out how to manage your identity), or aren't supposed to be in a casino for some reason, you should always give your name and address to anyone connected with the casino who asks. The casino wants your vital statistics so it can send you invitations to parties and promotions and give you free rooms and comped food. Give up your name and address if the pit boss or slot host asks for it. There's nothing to be afraid of.

I can't count the number of times someone has given this reason for deliberately not joining a slot club: "I don't want the casino to know how much I win or lose." The casino doesn't base its slot club benefits on your win/loss numbers (although it does keep records of it). Comp decisions are based mostly on the amount of money you put through the machine (original buy-in and winnings you're constantly churning back through, whether by coin or credit play). You *want* the casino to know that you put about $600-$700 an hour through a 25¢ video poker machine (about $4,800-$5,600 in a typical eight-hour day). That kind of action qualifies you (win or lose) for between $60 and $160 worth of slot club freebies, at most casinos, in the form of some combination of rooms, meals, cash, services, and gifts. Be paranoid if you must—but you're paying a high price for unnecessary privacy.

Myth Three
Casinos are apt to offer comps without being asked.

I've always been surprised by the number of people who have a fantasy of the eagle-eyed pit boss noticing their play and strolling over to say, "I can tell you're a player and the kind of customer our operation is looking for. Let me buy you lunch." It just doesn't happen to the low roller. Well, occasionally it will—you'll have been playing blackjack for ten hours and be all bleary-eyed and the pit boss will finally take pity on you and ask if you'd like a comp to the buffet. Of course, this is usually at two o'clock in the morning!

Just belonging to the slot club is no guarantee that you'll get everything you deserve. You might know that your points are worth comps, but a surprising number of casinos not only don't have printed literature on what the points are worth, but slot club booth personnel either don't know or are instructed not to volunteer the information. Some casinos operate differently. At the good ones, all you have to do is walk up to the booth and ask someone to look up your account. Then, if you qualify, a clerk writes a meal comp or refers you to a host. But even here, in almost all instances, the single-most valuable word in a casino, the critical three letters that have taken me farther in casinos than any others, are "A-S-K." You have to make them aware that you want something that you know you're entitled to.

Let me illustrate this important concept with two blackjack stories, one from our high-roller days and the other from our low-rolling.

Back when we were green-chip bettors, we were on a junket to a casino in Tahoe. We'd been playing for several days and it was time to check out. At the cashier, Brad asked if we had qualified to have our airfare reimbursed. The cashier said, "Yes," and handed him $600.

Another guy was standing next to Brad, and said, "I've lost $20,000 since Tuesday and I didn't get my airfare back." Brad said, "I bet you'd get your airfare back if you asked." The man did. After a call to a casino host, the cashier informed him that he qualified for the maximum reimbursement, peeled off ten $100 bills, and handed them over. This man had certainly had his room and meals comped, but he didn't know about airfare reimbursement and the casino wasn't volunteering to tell him. If it hadn't been for Brad, that man would have been permanently out that $1,000.

A similar episode occurred on the opposite side of the spectrum while we were playing $5 blackjack at Slots A Fun, a small casino next to Circus Circus in Las Vegas. It's a fun place to play $5 blackjack; a young low-roller crowd is attracted by the free Heineken (for players). We'd been playing several hours when I said jokingly to Brad, "I'm hungry. I wonder if they'll give us a comp to the snack bar." Slots A Fun serves those obscenely huge hot dogs, which only cost $1 in the first place, so I was laughing when I asked the pit boss, "Hey, have we played long enough to earn a comped hot dog?" I thought it was a joke right up until the time the boss said, "Sure! Are there just the two of you?" I said yes and he gave me an unlimited comp for two.

Well, we made a beeline for that snack bar and ran up a $25 tab. We helped ourselves to two of everything: shrimp cocktails, salads, chicken-finger dinners, drinks, and desserts. I had a Ziploc bag in my purse, into which I dumped the shrimp cocktails. When we got back to our room, I stashed it in our mini-refrigerator and we had a nice snack that night off the same comp—all because I'd asked the pit boss for a frankfurter.

Myth Four
Casinos cater more to table players than to slot players.

This used to be true. But these days, table players come to me and complain that they don't get treated as well playing green-chip blackjack and craps as the 25¢ machine players do. Or a wife who plays slots will get twice as many casino offers in the mail as her roulette-playing husband. Even when we played nothing higher than quarter video poker machines, we were invited to lavish parties with gourmet food, open bars, top-notch entertainment, expensive prizes, and complimentary photo sessions. In the lower-tier casinos, you can have hosts who come around, call you by name, and ask if you need anything.

Jeffrey Compton, slot club authority, quotes an amazing statistic: a $1 slot player is equivalent, in the casino's eyes, to a $100-per-hand blackjack player.

Even as quarter players we accumulated more food comps than we could possibly use. We got to participate in drawings that awarded great prizes (one time I won a Mercury Mystique). I got beauty salon comps and massages. We could get rooms when the hotels were full, even on short notice on holiday weekends; we could also get free rooms for our friends and family. Table players get fewer comps, proportional to the amount of money that they bet, than slot and video poker players who belong to, and know how to take advantage of, slot clubs.

Myth Five
*All casino personnel know
everything there is to know about gambling.*

This is a big fat "WRONG." I've been tendered more ill-informed, pea-brained, empty-headed information from casino employees than from anyone else in the world. I could probably write an entire book titled, "Bad Information I've Received From Casino Employees."

What's more, the higher you go up the chain of command, the worse it can get. One gambling magazine, overall a good one for consumers, used to publish a monthly column called "Executive Advice," in which they asked casino higher-ups to comment on various topics of interest to gamblers. I'm glad they eventually dropped that column, because I saw more downright fallacious information there, more just plain bad advice, than I'd ever seen in print—and by so-called experts.

The bone-headed information can run from the top to the bottom of the casino employee hierarchy. You can ask a change girl to show you a hot machine and she'll be happy to oblige, even though she has absolutely no idea what a "good" machine is or that there is no such thing as a "hot" machine. In most cases, all she's doing is showing 25 people 25 different machines in her area, hoping one of them hits so she'll get a big tip.

Many blackjack dealers will not only frown at you when you hit an A,7 against a face card, they'll ridicule you along with the rest of the table when you turn it into a hard 16 and bust, especially when he busts on the same hand. The dealer doesn't know that you played the hand perfectly according to the immutable laws of basic strategy.

I can't tell you the number of slot supervisors I've run across who couldn't tell me what comps I was entitled to.

I once asked an installer from the company that built the video poker machine I was playing to tell me the machine's payback percentage. He looked at me like I was speaking in Swahili. He had no idea what a payback percentage was.

When I first started gambling in casinos, I assumed that the people who worked there knew everything. I figured the blackjack dealers, for example, would know everything there was to know about blackjack. Wouldn't they have read all the books? Wouldn't they know if people were playing correctly? Heck no! I learned that blackjack dealers have all the same superstitions and addle-brained beliefs that most gamblers do. I used to think all the pit bosses knew how to count cards and how to recognize card counters. It's true that they're more knowledgeable today than they were 15-20 years ago, but even so, most pit bosses couldn't tell a card counter unless he came in wearing a sandwich board that read: "I am a card counter."

If you have to ask casino employees about something, such as the rules of a promotion or the times of an event, ask half a dozen of them and take a consensus of the answers. That'll provide you with some semblance of the facts.

Myth Six
People who play a lot, especially
locals, are knowledgeable about gambling.

Do not assume that people know what they're doing. Don't believe everything you hear from other players. The longer some people gamble, instead of wising up, the more entrenched they become in their misinformed ways. They take the bad information they learned initially and practice it so long that they believe it to be fact. Read the experts to get expert information (I've provided a list of the best resources about gambling on pg. 203).

That veteran gambler playing the video poker machine right next to you is likely to be full of well-meaning but bad advice. "Don't play that machine; it doesn't hit very often." Or, "Do play that machine; it's known to be a good payer." Or, "Play that five-coin machine, but only put in four coins at a time; it's programmed not to hit the royal if you play the fifth coin. It hits all the time with four. I know, I've seen it happen for months now." Or, "Don't play for the next three days. It's a holiday weekend and they've tightened up all the machines." (I often try to picture a mechanic with a screwdriver tightening up the "profit screw" when the casinos want to win more, and loosening it when the casinos decide to let the players win for a change.)

Blackjack players? Forget it! They'll give you advice all right. Verse number one: When a bad player sits down, leave right away, because he'll make the cards go bad. Same song, verse two: The third-base player must play "right," or else he'll ruin the whole table.

One roulette "expert" will tell you to bet red because it's come up black eight times in a row, while another will tell you to bet black because it's on a roll.

Likewise, crapshooters overflow with theories that are mathematically impossible.

A friend of mine who plays expert video poker tells a story about sitting down at a machine and playing five coins. A woman next to her says, "You must not play very much, honey." My friend says, "Well, I play quite a bit." The woman says, "Well, I'm a local. I play all the time. And it doesn't work to play five coins right away. You start with one coin and play a little while. Then go up to two coins, then three, then four, and only then is the machine primed to take five coins."

Once in a while, I might be the one sitting beside you. And if I like you and am feeling talkative, I might offer a little advice that might save you, or even make you, some money — but only if you ask. The key words are "if you ask." I used to try to be helpful to the people around me. If I saw them doing something awfully wrong, I would tell them that such and such was a better way. I don't do that anymore.

I learned my lesson early on when I was sitting beside a man playing a bonus Jacks or Better machine, on which you could choose the 4-of-a-kind you wanted for a bonus. This man had his machine set on four 3s for the bonus. I told him, "Sir, you might want to set the machine to pay the bonus on a face card instead of threes. You won't want to hold a single three, because a pair of threes doesn't pay anything. But a pair of jacks or queens or kings or aces will."

He replied indignantly, "Oh no. I'm really lucky with the threes. I've found that four threes comes up most often."

Well, I kind of slinked back to my own machine and thought to myself, that's the last time I ever try to help anyone who hasn't asked me for advice.

Myth Seven
*Anyone who writes about gambling
is an expert and can be counted on to give
100% accurate gaming advice.*

I don't want to mention any names of gambling authors and personalities who put out truly terrible information, but we can repeat some of the fallacies that they peddle to an unsuspecting public. I've read the advice of so-called experts who tell you never to split eights when you're playing blackjack if the dealer has a nine, ten, or ace showing. "You'll just end up with two eighteens that will both lose to the dealer's nineteen, twenty, or twenty-one," he says.

Well, blackjack basic strategy is not subject to debate. It's based on the results of billions of hands simulated by high-speed computers. If basic strategy says to always split eights and aces (which it does), that's exactly what you do, no matter what the dealer has showing, no matter what you had for dinner or what color shoes you're wearing, no matter that some snake-oil salesman tells you otherwise.

A friend of mine once went to a seminar where the speaker was asked if you should hit a soft 17 against a dealer's seven and he answered, "Sure, if you feel like it." My friend, knowing that this play is a solid basic-strategy hit, told me that she didn't believe another word that came out of the expert's mouth—and she'd paid good money to attend!

The same holds true with video poker. The strategies that have been worked out by computers are the only way to play. There is no argument for doing something in blackjack or video poker because you "feel" like doing it. Now, some strategies might be simplified and not cover every single minute contingency; this accounts for some strategies being slightly different than others. But when you run across something entirely out of line, such as the examples above, there's no justification for it. Once you know the truth, you quickly realize that not everybody who writes or lectures about gambling can be counted on to give accurate advice.

I'll tell you something else about strategies: there's also a powerful psychological reason to rely on computer-generated and tested plays. We'll talk about this in detail in Chapter Four, Video Poker.

Month in and month out, I see scads of ads in gambling magazines that talk about beating the slots by finding the hot machines, promising money-management systems that will make you a winner in negative-expectation games, influencing the dice by telekinesis, and other such nonsense. People are led to believe that they can use some sort of voodoo or crystal-ball gazing to win, then they go out and lose their hard-earned money plying these worthless techniques.

How can you tell if information is accurate? If you read widely, after a while you'll get a feel for what's right. After reading enough writers with mathematically sound premises, you'll be able to distinguish between the good and bad data. You'll learn that certain writers can be trusted. But be careful; the same doesn't always hold true for periodicals. Some magazines have good articles on some subjects, but other articles are suspect as to their validity. If you're new to gambling, you need to have a healthy amount of skepticism. I can help you here; I've read most of the periodicals that are out on the market. Any book, magazine, or newsletter you see in the Resources list, you can count on providing good information.

2

Great Expectations
A Reality Check

The Pyramid of Gamblers

For years, skeptics have been buttonholing Brad and me about our gambling. "You must lose a lot of money to be treated like VIPs," they say. "Otherwise, how could you get all those free rooms and meals? The casinos always win in the long run; how else could they pay for all those lights?" They simply cannot believe that we do what we say we do.

Other people have genuinely wanted to learn from our experiences, but they're looking for a 25-words-or-less answer to their questions. It was our frustration over the people seeking the quick road to casino riches that was most responsible for this book being born.

I began thinking about all the people who go to casinos and why they go there, and I came up with two fundamental reasons: monetary gain and entertainment. Considering these goals, I came up with a four-level pyramid, which I've found useful for sorting out types of gamblers. This pyramid has helped me show others how to go into a casino as smarter gamblers, which often leads to coming out of a casino as happier gamblers.

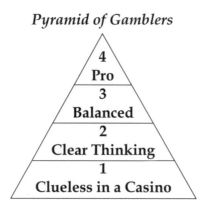

Pyramid of Gamblers

4
Pro
3
Balanced
2
Clear Thinking
1
Clueless in a Casino

Level 4—Room at the Top

The pointed apex of the pyramid—Level 4—represents the few professional gamblers who've made the casinos their place of employment. This includes some extremely knowledgeable computer-savvy race and sports bettors, some skilled blackjack card counters, and live poker and video poker experts. For these true professionals, gambling is their only source of income: they work very hard and often put in much more than the standard 40-hour work week.

Still on Level 4, but under the full-time pro, is a group of casino customers who play at a professional level, but don't rely on gambling winnings for their sole support. Most in this group think of gambling as their part-time job, using winnings to supplement pensions or income from other sources. These people may enjoy their "job" and, thus, are also entertained, but their main purpose in the casino is to make money. This book may give someone who aspires to be a peak-of-the-gambling-pyramid professional a few starter ideas, but it's not written for Level 4 players. It's written to help those in the lower levels who want to move higher.

Level 1 — The Broad Base

Let's skip down to Level 1, which contains the largest group of gamblers. I call them "The Confused." You see them in every casino, wandering around in a wild-eyed daze, frustrated in their search for a "win." Some sit stoically at one machine for hours, muttering that the machine has to hit because it has so much of their money inside it. Others rush from table to table, hunting for a "lucky" one. Others are up in their rooms where they're trying to figure out how they could have lost so much money so fast.

You could also call these gamblers the "I-Don't-Know-Why-I'm-Here" bunch, because they have never really thought about their goals when they enter a casino. You can ask anyone who goes into a casino if he wants to win and you'll get a strong "Of course." But ask him if he usually does win, and he'll probably start laughing too hard to even get out a "No." Investigating further, you ask, "Well, if you usually lose, then why are you here?" At this point, most people are at a loss for words. They might stutter something like, "Well, I'm hoping to get lucky this time," or mumble, "I feel a jackpot coming on."

You really have to pin people down to get them to admit that they are in a casino because they're having fun, in spite of the likelihood that they'll lose. I believe this comes from the traditional image of gambling as a vice. Many people still feel guilty when they lose money in a casino.

We have a couple of friends who go to Las Vegas, stay in nice $35 hotel rooms that would cost them more than $100 in any other major city, eat $25 prime rib dinners for the cost of the tip to the waiter, and spend three days enjoying spectacular pirate battles, exploding volcanos, laser-light shows, circus acts, and unlimited drinks — all free. Then they moan about "wasting" (losing) $100 in the nickel slots. They just can't admit that having fun was their primary goal.

Level 2 — Enlightenment Strikes

All it takes is a little shift in perspective to climb the short ladder to Level 2. *Winning* isn't the name of the game. *Entertainment* is. I think we all know that, at heart. You've heard the same comments that I have: "I spent all evening on the riverboat and only lost twenty-five dollars — I had a great time." And "We spent an entire week in Biloxi, MS, this year and even though we lost $1,000, the vacation cost us much less than three days at Disney World." Recently, Brad talked to a couple from California who've been going to Las Vegas for 20 years. "We've never really won," they told him with good humor. "But we just love it there."

So the first thing you must do to raise yourself above the confusion of Level 1 is to analyze your goals for your casino excursions. Although beating the casino might be at the forefront of your thinking, take care to factor in entertainment and give it its proper value.

"Okay," you say, "I admit that, for me, casino gambling is a recreational activity." Now, by keeping it within the entertainment context, you can better consider the money factor. That is, you realize that you get a lot of entertainment value for your money, but you would like your bankroll to provide more hours of this entertainment — which means winning more often and/or losing less during your time in the casino.

A warning note is in order here. We're assuming

your gambling bankroll (the money you take to the casino to gamble) is money you can afford to spend (lose) on casino entertainment. This is not the rent or mortgage payment. This isn't the baby's milk money. This isn't money you've borrowed or should be saving. Your bankroll should come from discretionary funds — money that, if it's lost, will not negatively impact your lifestyle or cause a financial hardship to you or your family, now or in the future. No gambler at any level should enter a casino and risk money that's needed for living expenses. To do so is to court disaster, not just financially, but emotionally as well. One can never be truly "entertained" when gambling with money earmarked for other purposes.

There is another group of gamblers within Level 1 that needs to evaluate closely what they're doing. They're not just confused, they're angry, too. They can *never* lose money gambling and chalk up the losses to entertainment. They cannot accept even a small loss without being devastated. These players have told me, "When I lose, even if I can afford it, I get physically ill. I have this sinking feeling in the pit of my stomach the whole time I'm in a casino." If gambling can provide no entertainment value for you, then you should stay far away from casinos. Even the pros at the top of the pyramid lose for long stretches at a time between their winning sessions. The only sure thing about gambling results is that they are streaky — if you're susceptible to motion sickness, don't get on the roller coaster.

Some Arithmetic

Even though Level 2 players feel that entertainment is their primary goal in a casino, they have monetary goals too — winning more and/or losing less so their entertainment can last longer. But before I can teach you to be a clear-thinking gambler, you have to know at least a little about odds. Having been a high-school English teacher for more years than I care to disclose, I could always handle words better than numbers. Math was never one of my strong suits. It may not be yours either. But you have to understand some of the basics. The most important thing to understand is the difference between a *negative-expectation* and a *positive-expectation* gambling game. I'll be using these two terms throughout the book, so let's talk about them right off the bat.

First, the math. If you put a hundred dollars into a slot machine, and the machine is programmed, over the long run, to give you your hundred dollars back, you are playing an even game. It has neither negative nor positive expectation. If, however, for every $100 you put into the machine, you get back only $97, then the casino has a 3% advantage. This is known as a negative-expectation game (for the player, of course). On the other hand, if you play a machine that, for every $100 played, gives back $101 over the long haul, then *you* have an edge of 1%. This is called a positive-expectation game.

Most of the games in a casino are negative-expectation games. This means that no matter what you do, whatever strategy you employ, whatever money-management system you use, in the long run you will lose when you play them. I'm not trying to discourage you from playing them. I'm simply making you aware of the incontrovertible mathematical realities of gambling when it comes to the majority of games on the casino floor. When you gamble at negative-expectation games, *you are the underdog.*

However, there are a few machines or games where you can get into positive-expectation territory. These games are structured in such a way that playing skillfully can reverse the situation and make you the favorite when you play them. You can lose on any one day, week, month, or even year, but if you play a positive-expectation game long enough, eventually you can come out ahead.

Keep in mind that these positive and negative percentages hold true over the long run. The results are often different in the short term. In any session you can

---

Positive-Expectation Games

When played skillfully, the games listed below may yield positive expectation.

Blackjack   Sports Betting
Poker   Video Poker
Race Betting

Potentially Positive

Any game played in a tournament format.
Any game with a progressive feature or an
    equity consideration.
Any game played with a coupon.
Any game played as part of a special pro-
    motion.
Any game associated with a slot club or
    similar rebate program.
Any game when comps are factored in.

Negative-Expectation Games

Baccarat   Pai Gow
Bingo   Pai Gow Poker
Caribbean Stud Poker   Red Dog
Craps   Roulette
Keno   Slot Machines
Let It Ride   War

Also, all games listed in Positive Expectation when played at average skill levels.

play a negative-expectation game and win, or play a positive-expectation game and lose. If you play long enough, however, the math will bear out, albeit slowly, to the expected result: positive or negative.

Why is knowing about odds and game expectation so important? Because the casino edge represents the "cost" for your casino entertainment. You have to know the various costs in order to choose the best value for your money. It's a little like comparison shopping at several supermarkets.

The Price to Play

How much you lose while gambling is not determined solely by the casino advantage. The size and number of your wagers, along with how well you play a game, are equally important. Anthony Curtis once wrote a great article on this subject for *Casino Player* magazine and came up with the invaluable charts that follow. The charts take into consideration all of the factors just mentioned to derive a good approximation of what it costs to play each game. The key word is "approximation." It was necessary for Anthony to estimate some of the variables; he also rounded the results for user friendliness.

The charts analyze 46 wagers from 10 different games. For a quick assessment of what your favorite game costs to play, locate it, and jump to the far right-hand column in the chart. The figure there is the approximate dollar-per-hour loss you can expect (when playing at a minimum bet level and average speed). For those who want to use these fascinating charts to explore other betting scenarios, I've included Anthony's full explanation of the entries (pg. 23) to facilitate your fiddling.

It's important to keep in mind that neither the ap-

plication of expert strategies for the beatable games
(like blackjack and video poker), nor givebacks (like
slot club cashback and comps) have been considered
here. We will concentrate heavily on both throughout
this book to eliminate some "casino costs."

BACCARAT

	casino advantage	hands per hour	standardized measure	wager amount	cost per hour of play
Baccarat					
bank	1.06%	80	.85	$100	$ 85
player	1.24	80	.99	100	99
tie	14.40	80	11.49	2	287
Mini Baccarat					
bank	1.06%	130	1.38	5	7
player	1.24	130	1.61	5	8
tie	14.40	130	18.67	1	19

BLACKJACK

	casino advantage	hands per hour	standardized measure	wager amount	cost per hour of play
Basic Strategy					
1 deck	.0%	60	0.00	$ 5	$ 0
2 decks	.3	60	.18	5	1
4,6 decks	.5	60	.30	5	2
8 decks	.6	60	.36	5	2
Avg. Player	2.0	60	1.20	5	6
Poor Player	3.5	60	2.10	5	11

SLOTS

	casino advantage	hands per hour	standardized measure	wager amount	cost per hour of play
nickle slots	9.0%	400	36	15¢	$ 5
quarter slots	7.5	400	30	75¢	22
dollar slots	4.5	400	18	$ 3	54

CRAPS

	casino advantage	hands per hour	standardized measure	wager amount	cost per hour of play
Line/Odds/Place					
pass/don't pass	1.4%	30	.42	$ 5	$ 2
w/single odds	.8	30	.24	5	2
w/double odds	.6	30	.18	5	2
place 6 or 8	1.5	30	.45	6	2
Field					
pay 2x on 12	5.6	100	5.55	5	28
pay 3x on 12	2.8	100	2.77	5	14
Multi-roll Prop					
hardway 6 or 8	9.1%	30	2.73	1	3
Single-roll Prop					
any 7	16.7%	100	16.67	1	17

VIDEO POKER

	casino advantage	hands per hour	standardized measure	wager amount	cost per hour of play
Jacks or Better					
5¢ (6/5)	5.0%	500	25.0	25¢	$ 6
25¢ (8/5)	2.7	500	13.5	$1.25	17
25¢ (9/6)	.5	500	2.5	1.25	3
Bonus Poker					
25¢ (8/5)	.8	500	4.0	1.25	5
Atlantic City					
25¢ (Joker)	2.8	500	14.0	1.25	18
Average Player					
25¢ (Jacks/Bonus)	3.0	500	15.0	1.25	19
25¢ (Wild Cards)	4.0	500	20.0	1.25	25

KENO & SPORTS

	casino advantage	hands per hour	standardized measure	wager amount	cost per hour of play
Keno					
1 spot	25%	7	1.75	$ 1	$ 2
2-15 spot	30	7	2.10	1	2
Video Keno					
5¢	15%	300	45.0	20¢	9
25¢	8	300	24.0	1	24
Sports Betting					
Bet $11/win $10	4.5%	.5	.02	11	25¢

NEWER GAMES					
	casino advantage	hands per hour	standardized measure	wager amount	cost per hour of play
Caribbean Stud					
ante	5.3%	40	2.12	$ 5	$ 11
bonus	48.0	40	19.2	1	19
Let It Ride					
base bet	3.5%	40	1.4	5	7
bonus bet	45.0	40	18.4	1	18

ROULETTE					
	casino advantage	hands per hour	standardized measure	wager amount	cost per hour of play
single zero	2.70%	50	1.35	$ 5	$ 7
double zero	5.26	50	2.63	5	13
Atlantic City					
outside (dbl. 0)	2.63	50	1.32	5	7

Casino Advantage — The casino advantage for most games is known. In places where the advantage is variable (blackjack and video poker), there are multiple assignments. In the case of slot machines, the payback percentages were extrapolated from published win figures for Las Vegas casinos. Slot returns in Las Vegas are traditionally higher than in other casino areas, so you might have to increase the casino edge by a percentage point or two when evaluating machines in other parts of the country.

Hands Per Hour — This measure will be affected by playing conditions, most significantly the number of players on the game. Crowded conditions produce the slowest rate of play, which is desirable on negative-expectation games, since every bet you make adds to the cost of gambling. The chart estimates hands per hour according to full-table conditions and for a casual rate of play on machines. If you find that you're playing faster than the speeds listed, you'll be losing at a rate faster than the charts indicate in the "Cost per Hour" entry.

Standardized Measure (SM) — The standardized measure combines the effects of the house edge and the speed of the games (it's derived by multiplying those two figures). The lower the SM, the less costly the game is to play *assuming the bet size is the same*. A player who wants to wager a set amount per hand, say $100, can go down the chart comparing SMs to determine that craps (.42) is better than baccarat (.85), that keno (1.75) is better than Caribbean Stud (2.12), and so on. The lowest SM on the chart is 0 for single-deck blackjack with basic strategy. The highest is 68.75 for the progressive sidebet on the video version of Caribbean Stud.

Wager Amount — The wager amount listed in the chart is the minimum that the game can generally be played for. In some games (craps with odds, Caribbean Stud, Let It Ride), you will frequently have more money in action than the listed minimum. Don't worry about that; it's been accounted for in the calculations.

Cost Per Hour — This is it. The bottom line. Your ticket price for one hour's worth of gambling entertainment. The cost per hour is calculated by multiplying the SM by the "Wager Amount." You can easily calculate the cost for betting more than the minimum by multiplying the SM by the amount of your average bet. Example: If you bet $3 one-spot keno tickets, the cost per hour is 1.75 x $3 = $5.25 per hour.

What to Play

You decide on your personal goals. No one can tell you what you ought to play. If the game you play isn't particularly important to you and you just want to soak up the casino ambience as long as possible, you might choose sports betting with its low 25¢-an-hour cost. Or maybe you like the high of knowing that if you play Megabucks, for example, you might hit a life-changing jackpot; you don't care that you won't be able to play as long (because the casino advantage is higher for slots with enormous jackpots). Or perhaps you want to play only video poker, but as long as possible on your limited bankroll; so you choose a machine with a better payback schedule. Or you love the excitement of the dice table, but you go broke too quickly; so you decide to switch from field betting to the pass line to make your gambling sessions last longer.

If you study the charts and start choosing better bets, you will put yourself solidly on Level 2—the area of clear thinking.

Money Management

Now is a good time to discuss money management. Almost every gambling book you read has a big section on this subject. Some of the information can be useful, but much of it is little more than a cruel hoax. Proponents of money-management often promise something that's impossible: using a betting system to turn negative expectation into positive expectation. Some of these systems sellers would have you believe that you can trick the math and turn a losing game into a winning one simply by making a complicated series of wagers. Many money-management systems have the characteristic of enhancing your chances of winning (small amounts) over the short term, but in the long run they're still losers. Skill in playing, not betting, is what determines your expected result.

The one kind of money-management system that does make some sense is dividing your gambling bankroll to avoid losing everything in one session. Remember, at this stage we're taking steps to make our gambling stake last longer. If your bankroll is limited, there's nothing wrong with dividing it by some pre-determined number to correspond with the number of sessions you think you'll play. For example, let's say you're going to Biloxi. You'll be staying three days and you're bringing $3,000. You could divide first by the number of days. On the first day, take $1,000 and put the other $2,000 away. Now, let's say you plan to play once in the morning, once in the afternoon, and once in the evening. You can further divide your $1,000 into $333 for each playing session. As far as I'm concerned, it's all right to take the whole grand and risk it in the morning. If you blow it all, you'll just have to find something else to do in the afternoon and evening of that first day. But I believe most people would rather divvy up the money into three piles of $333 so their scheduled gambling sessions are ensured.

If you lose the first $333 pile in the morning, your next move is pretty clear cut: you quit playing and spend your time eating, lying on the beach, sightsee-ing, or engaged in some other non-gambling activity. But what if you come back in the afternoon with the second $333 and break even after three hours? Some people quit and put that $333 away and never touch it, figuring that they've "won" it (or at least haven't lost it) that session. If one of your goals is to not lose the entire bankroll for your trip, then go ahead and lock it up to take home. Otherwise, add it to your remaining trip money as a sort of gambling reserve.

You do the same in the evening, and on the second day, and on the third day. Remember, this "system" will not improve your chances of winning in any way. It just provides some discipline in managing your bankroll and making it last, so you can gamble the whole time you're at the casino. It's no fun to be broke and still have two days of your casino vacation left.

Gambling purists might scoff at this suggestion, but remember, we're still at Level 2. Consider the following story.

Husband-and-wife friends of ours once planned a three-day trip to Las Vegas. They sat on the airplane for four hours, then caught a taxi to their hotel where they encountered a long line at check-in. The wife agreed to wait in the line while the husband went to shoot craps (a negative-expectation game). About half an hour later, he returned to find his wife at the counter, ready to check in. "Never mind getting the key," he said. "I just lost all our money." They left the hotel, went back to the airport, put their names on a stand-by list, and flew home the same day. They never even made it to their hotel room! Even the purists would find it hard to argue that our friends' vacation wouldn't have benefitted from some sensible money management.

Level 3—Getting Your Balance

You may be forever satisfied to stay at Level 2—many people are. They budget their gambling bankroll carefully. They know what casino games they enjoy and the costs of playing them. When they have a winning session, they're thrilled. When they lose, they say, "We had fun—that's what's important."

But some of you may want to go up to Level 3. I call this the "Balanced" level, the level at which the monetary goal becomes as important as the entertainment goal. Maybe, as in our own case, you want the "fun factor" to last longer than it should given your bankroll. Or maybe the fun for you comes from the winning, not just from playing the game.

Regardless, to reach Level 3 you'll have to work a bit. You'll have to study. You'll have to bother with details. There's no magic pill that will instantly vault you to this playing status. But don't despair. The next several chapters of this book are chock full of helpful hints that we have discovered on our successful 20-year journey into the land of endless casino "fun." Take my hand and I'll guide you to the top of Level 2 and, if you're serious, up to Level 3. We'll take it slow—the incline is too steep to go fast.

3

Slot Machines
Handle With Care

There's an old gambling story about a crapshooter whose wife, a slot player, walks up to him at the crap table to tell him that she needs more money.

"What happened to that hundred dollars I gave you?" he asks.

When she says, "I lost it," he starts berating her for playing the slots.

"Well, I've been playing for three hours and having lots of fun," she responds. "You've been playing craps now for three hours. How much have you lost?"

"Oh, I'm down a couple thousand, but I know how to gamble!"

Slot players get a bad rap. Many table game players look down on machine players. This is pretty funny to me, because many machine players are bucking a smaller casino edge (on a per-pull basis) than the table gamblers. While (dollar) slot players typically face a 3%-5% edge, compare that with the other charts on pgs. 21-23: a 30% edge at keno, a 9%-16% edge on a lot of the bets on a crap table, a 10%-20% edge on the big six, even a 5.3% edge at the roulette wheel. Of course, the chart shows that speed of play is a huge factor in expected losses playing the slots. But the fact is, almost any dollar slot player in Las Vegas is battling a lower hourly expected loss than a $25 roulette player.

What's worse, a surprising number of table game mavens don't differentiate between slot players and video poker players. They think that if it's a machine with a slot that takes a coin, it's a slot machine. In this book, I never say "slot" machine when I mean "video poker" machine.

Video poker players also tend to look down on slot players. This is also funny to me, because I know lots of knowledgeable video poker players who willingly play less-than-100%-return machines when they are the only ones available. And the truth is, many slot players feeding a machine and accruing slot club points are doing better than a lot of casual video poker players who give back much of the potential return from video poker due to poor play.

The problem is, table game and video poker snobs just don't understand differences in the goals of gamblers. Since one out of two casino gamblers is a slot player, the slots must be providing something of value to their devotees. And they are. What is it? Again, it's entertainment. Slot players aren't in a casino to make an hourly wage. They want to have fun. If they win, good for them. But while they're losing, they want to have a good time doing it. The bright lights, spinning reels, coins clinking, and drinks flowing, along with the anticipation of getting lucky and hitting the big jackpot, all add up to excitement and entertainment.

And that's just fine with me. Don't worry that I'll try to convert all slot players to positive-expectation video poker. Read on and I'll show you how you can keep more money in your pocket and out of the clutches of the casino, and still have an all-around good time. I'll show you how to be a clear-thinking slot player, having a blast on Level 2 of the gambling pyramid.

"Library Skills" for Slot Players

If you want to play the slots, the first thing you must do is learn to "read" the machines. I'm not talking about some hokey method of targeting which one is about to pay off — there is no legitimate way to do that. I'm talking about gathering what information is available about the machines to determine which ones have the attributes you're looking for. A gambling machine is like a book: you must understand what it's about before you can determine if you want to pay attention to it. As you do when you select reading material at a bookstore, you need to browse the machines that you might want to play.

There are hundreds of different kinds of slot machines, but you can always recognize them because they have "reels" instead of playing cards (which are found on video poker and video blackjack machines) or numbers (which are found on video keno machines). There are usually three or four reels (or columns) of images of fruit, or sevens, or other symbols. (The Four Queens in downtown Las Vegas used to have the largest slot machine in the world — with eight reels across — until they junked it.)

Nowadays, you have to study machines a little more carefully, because with the advent of video slots, the reels appear as images on a screen rather than as real reels. To confuse you even further, the popular multi-game machines let you choose among keno, blackjack, video poker, and reel slots, all with only a push of a menu button. And just recently I saw a machine that is the ultimate in confusion for the student gambler: a video poker machine that gives you a bonus determined by spinning reels.

As in all gambling games, the first thing you need to check is the minimum. That is, how much you have to bet. I see it all the time: a player walks up to a dollar machine and puts a quarter into it. The quarter goes right through and clanks into the tray, and the player stands there puzzled for a moment before realizing that it's a dollar machine. I've also seen people trying to put five nickels into a quarter machine or two quarters into a fifty-cent machine. That's a little more logical, but it still doesn't work. It's not as embarrassing as laying down a $5 chip on a $100-minimum blackjack table, but you'll still feel a bit sheepish when the people around you see you make this mistake.

So read the machine. Whether it takes pennies, nickels, dimes, quarters, fifty-cent pieces, or dollar, five dollar, twenty-five dollar, hundred dollar, or even five-hundred dollar tokens will be denoted somewhere on the machine. You might have to hunt; sometimes the denomination isn't clearly marked. If it's not, you can usually tell by looking at the size of the coin slot: the slot for dollar tokens is much wider than the slot for quarters, which is bigger than the slot for nickels.

The second thing to look for is how many coins the machine takes and whether or not it pays proportionally. On some machines it doesn't matter how many coins you put in. If you play one quarter and hit one cherry, you get 25¢ back. If you play four quarters and get one cherry, you get $1 back. Five quarters and one cherry returns $1.25. Whether you play one or five coins on that machine, the payoffs are proportionally equal.

Many reel machines, however, pay differently. On some machines, you'll be ineligible to win the highest jackpot unless you play maximum coins. Following a strategy of playing max coins on these types of slot machines is more about psychological well-being than anything else. Nothing is more demoralizing than hitting the highest symbol combination on one of these machines with fewer than the maximum coins played. I once walked by a row of four vacant Megabucks machines and checked to see how much the last player at each machine had bet: two had bet the three $1 tokens that made them eligible to hit the jackpot ($7 million at the time); one had played a single dollar token; the other had put in two dollar tokens. If one of the latter two players had lined up the four Megabucks symbols on the bottom line, do you think they could have been content with their $5,000 or $10,000 win and never wondered "what if?" If you want to play "short-coin" on a slot machine, choose one with proportional pay-offs — and call it emotional insurance.

Pay close attention to the pay particulars of "7s" machines; they can be tricky. We were in a casino one day and a woman started yelling, "I got three blue sevens! I got three blue sevens!" We looked over and sure enough, there they were, three blue 7s lined up on the pay line. However, there were no lights flashing, no bells ringing, no credits racking up, no money coming out of the machine. The woman cried, "Where's my jackpot?" Upon closer inspection, we saw that with less-than-max coins played, payoffs were limited to bars and cherries only; to get paid for 7s you had to have three coins in. The woman had played two coins, so when her three blue 7s came up, instead of winning a $1,000 jackpot, she got nothing.

As it turned out, the woman didn't have to wait long for her redemption. Brad explained to her that she had to play three coins to get paid for that hand, and then the weirdest thing happened. The woman plunked in three coins and you could've knocked us over with a feather—the three blue 7s came up again! All I could think was that there must be a gambling god someplace that sometimes takes pity on poor gamblers.

Small Pots or Longshots?

Another good thing to know about a slot machine before you play it is whether it's a "frequent-pay" or a "big-jackpot" machine. If you're playing Quartermania, for example, you only have to play two quarters to win a $1 million or $2 million jackpot. But because a lot of money has to go into the machine to build up the big prize, Quartermania pays out fewer smaller jackpots. This means that unless you're one of the chosen few (very few!) who hit the headline-making pot of gold, you figure to lose at a faster rate than on machines with lower top-end prizes.

Conversely, some quarter machines have a top jackpot of only $100 or $200 or $500. The top jackpot is low, so you'll get more smaller jackpots along the way, and stay in the game longer.

Some people like to hear the coins drop into the tray or see the credits rack up more frequently. Other people are playing for that lifestyle-changing jackpot, like Cool Millions where you're paid $1 million on the spot, or the other "linked progressives" like Megabucks, Fabulous Fifties, Quartermania, and Nevada Nickels where you're paid umpteen thousands of dollars for the next 20 or 25 years. Which one you go after—the small but frequent payouts or the mother of all jackpots—is entirely your choice, but you need to be aware of how it will affect your playing sessions. The rule of thumb is: the larger the high-end jackpot, the less often you will have small wins.

Slot Machine Odds

One of the most frequent questions I'm asked is, "How do I know which slot machine will give me the best odds?" Unlike video poker (as you'll see in the next chapter), determining slot machine odds is not an exact science. Far from it. Back in the "good old days" when slot machines were mechanical, you could count the number of symbols on each reel and calculate the payback percentages. Nowadays, most slot machines are computerized, allowing each casino to set the paybacks at whatever percentages they want to. It no longer has anything to do with the number of reels and the number of symbols that you see on each reel.

Most people don't know this, but the reels themselves are just the physical manifestation, the expression, of what's called a "random number generator." Frank Scoblete, a prolific gambling writer, calls it "the god in the machine," which is an interesting way to visualize it. The reels are something to watch to make the game exciting and enjoyable, but the odds are already set. If the casino decides, for example, that it wants to take 3% of the action on a machine, it means that over the long haul that machine can be counted on to hold on to pretty close to 3% of the money played through it. And the random number generator sees to it that the money is won randomly. That's important. It's the reason that all those machine-selection-based slot systems you read about don't work. Machines don't become due, or hot, or played out. Nor do they lapse into predictable cycles. They pay (or don't pay) randomly.

Do casinos set different return rates? Sure they do. The way a casino sets the payback percentage depends on a number of business determinations: the desired profit margin, the sophistication of the customers, and the competition, among others. The problem is, there's no way for you to know what those percentages are. The same machine that a Strip megaresort sets for a 3% hold could be set for a 7% hold in one of the grind joints in downtown Las Vegas or for a 10% hold on a riverboat in Missouri. All the machines look exactly alike, so there's no way to determine this just by looking at the machine; only the casino knows.

Still, you can use a few general rules based on facts to guide you. Because the casinos in Atlantic City have to publish their slot machine win figures, charts that tell you how much each casino in Atlantic City paid out on its quarter machines, fifty-cent machines, dollar machines, etc. are reprinted every month in magazines like *Casino Player*. The New Jersey casinos don't differentiate between video poker and slots, but you can still get an idea. The *Casino Player* charts also cover slot payouts in Connecticut, Nevada, Illinois, Iowa, Colorado, Mississippi, Indiana, and Missouri. They give you a good total picture of the slot scene in the U.S.

The charts show other things, too. For example, the higher the coin denomination of the slot machine, the higher the payback. This is almost always true in any casino. The payback percentage from a 5¢ or 25¢ machine will rarely be as high as a $1 or $5 machine. Why? Because the casino can take a small portion of a big bet and still make just as much money, if not more, than a big portion of a small bet. The casino can take only 2% of a $1 bet and make its 2¢, but it has to take 20% of a nickel bet to make a penny. As a rule, the higher the denomination of the machine, the lower the percentage the casino takes.

Here's another rule of thumb. Economics dictates that bigger casinos are likely to offer higher return percentages. It's the same idea as above: a smaller piece of a bigger pie. A big casino with lots of players can afford to give back more than a smaller casino with less volume.

The casino's location can also be used as a gauge. If you play 25¢ slots in Atlantic City, as a general rule the return is 92% at the best casino. So for every $100 you put into the best slot machine in Atlantic City, you can expect to lose on average $8. It's known that Las Vegas has higher slot paybacks than most, if not all, other casino venues, due to the extreme competition in the granddaddy of all gambling locales. Within Las Vegas, the downtown casinos in general pay back a slightly higher percentage (nearly 96%) than the Strip casinos. These are averages. There may be a casino on the Strip that has higher slot machine payback percentages than one of the tougher casinos downtown. In general, though, you'll lose a little more slowly playing slots in downtown Las Vegas than you will on the Strip or in Atlantic City, and probably significantly more slowly than in any other casino jurisdiction.

One more point. You'll see big signs in the casinos, particularly on the $1 slot machines, that claim, "These machines pay back up to 97%." I've seen them up as high as 99%. But don't be fooled. Since the sign says *up to* 97%, there may be one machine in that bank that pays 97%, while the rest pay much less.

You might ask, "Why couldn't casinos give you back 80% instead of 97%? Why wouldn't they want to earn 20% instead of just 3%?" Well, after a while, the players (particularly the locals and those who go to casinos frequently) would realize that they were losing all the time and quickly. They'd eventually go next door, or across the street, or wherever they could enjoy more gamble for their buck. People do get a feel for how much they lose and they can pretty much tell the difference—if the difference is large enough.

I hope you've noticed that all the return percentages quoted above are below 100%, and realize, accordingly, that if you play long enough, you will lose. You can almost never finish ahead of the slot machines after long periods of play—unless you get very very lucky and hit a huge jackpot. And even if you do hit a big payday, you can lose. I heard a story about a slot player who hit a jackpot of more than a million dollars, and within two years he'd poured all of his winnings back in.

You Can Go "Reel-less"

Although the reel slots (and video poker) are by far the most common gambling machines in the casino, there are other kinds. My overall view of reel slot machines holds true for every gambling machine that you'll find in a casino except video poker: you probably can't beat it. But you'll find plenty of video blackjack and video keno, as well as the new video Let It Ride and Caribbean Stud machines, so let's take a quick look.

Video blackjack machines aren't very popular and don't have much of a presence in casinos. No great loss. With rare exceptions, you won't encounter a blackjack machine that's beatable over the long run. Once in a blue moon you'll bump into one that comes close to paying back 100%, and with slot club benefits you might be able to break even. But even when you do find one, it requires a high level of blackjack knowledge for you to exploit successfully.

Video keno machines, on the other hand, are popular, and you'll find them everywhere. Keno machines are exciting to a lot of players. The problem with them is twofold: they pay poorly and they play fast—a combination that takes your money more quickly than even some of the worst reel slots (check the charts on pg. 21

and 22 again). You're far better off playing live keno with its much more leisurely pace. (Just a thought. I know that live keno holds a certain appeal for gamblers who want to keep the action going while they eat lunch, have a drink, or just take a break. But if the casino put signs on the keno boards similar to those on slot machines that said, "This Game Pays Back Up To 65%," do you think it would be so popular?)

Video Let It Ride (LIR) and video Caribbean Stud (CS)? Well, you *might* see them around in the future, but I wouldn't bet on it. The combination of casino advantage and speed of play in these games is even more deadly than in video keno (especially if you make the LIR and CS bonus bets). These games debuted at the dollar level and the public would have none of it. Then the machines were retrofitted to accept quarters, but that hasn't helped, either. Much like keno, the live versions of these games have the redeeming quality of being social gambling games. Not so the video versions.

Whoa, Nellie!

While we're on the subject, let's take another look at speed. The speed factor is an important consideration for all slot players. Any time you're playing a negative-expectation game, the slower you play, the less you lose. Anything you can do to slow down your play is a good idea. Some people bounce from machine to machine. Some people cash out their credits and feed the coins in by hand. Some people spin the reels ten times, then stop and take a sip of their drink or look at the action around them. Don't use the bill feeder; wait for the change person to come along. Instead of slavishly pushing buttons for three hours straight, try pulling handles, and take your time doing it. Converse with friends. Think of other ways to amuse yourself while you're sitting in front of a slot machine.

Do you want to calculate the benefits of slowing it down? Let's consider the long-term loss per hour on a reel slot machine with the whopping 97% return that the casinos seem so proud of. On a machine with a maximum-coin bet of 75¢ and slow play (300 pulls per hour), you're putting through $225 per hour. Three percent of that is only $6.75 an hour. On the same quarter machine with a 97% return and fast play (500 pulls an hour), your expected loss per hour rises quickly—to $11.25. How about slow play on a $1 machine with three tokens played that pays back, say, 95%? Your expected loss is $45 an hour. Fast play on the same machine? You'd better sit down, because you can expect to lose at a rate of $75 an hour.

The moral? If you must play negative-expectation games, play them slowly. You'll get more drinks, you'll soak up more casino ambience, and you'll get more of your money's worth in entertainment pleasure.

Beating the New Breed

I never thought I'd see a slot machine I liked, since I don't like any gambling activity where I don't have an advantage of some sort. Well, that was until I met the pigs. Piggy Bankin' was one of the first "new generation" slot machines unveiled in late 1996. It featured a series of cartoon antics by a piggy bank that talked and oinked to you. They were fun to play and were springing up on riverboats and casinos all over the country. When you lined up three blanks on the reels, your bet went into the "piggy bank," a progressive jackpot that grew until a "break the bank" symbol stopped on the last reel. When the bank was broken, the jackpot was added to your credits and the bank reset at 10 coins.

As soon as Piggy Bankin' appeared in casinos, the pros calculated that it became a positive-expectation game if you played only one coin at a time, and played only when the piggy bank held 25 coins or more. Not playing max coins knocked you out of the running for the top two bonus jackpots (and you'd miss what I've heard is a very good pig impression of Elvis). But you were better off playing just the single coin.

We "checked the pigs" at all the casinos we visited to see if we could find one with 25 or more coins in the bank. Occasionally, we stumbled on a real find, one with 50 or more. Like all gambling endeavors, even positive ones, we didn't come out ahead on every pig, but we were well ahead of the game overall. We won more than $400 one winter by doing a long "piggy run" up and down the Strip and around downtown during one of our exercise routines.

For a couple of years, many other of these new-generation slot machines showed up, with similar game-within-a-game bonus features, sophisticated video animation, and sharp, ultra-high-resolution, 3-D graphics. These machines became very popular with slot lovers, but the manufacturers were soon forced to make major changes to the bonusing element. A few "vultures" were spoiling it for everyone, employing aggressive, even threatening, behavior to try to force regular players off machines that had high bonuses ready to be plucked. Although there are still some bonusing slot machines that go positive once in a while, this bonus-hunting activity is not as lucrative as it once was.

However, there's been no let-up in the technological advances and creativity that slot machine manufacturers are continually investing in their products. If you think I haven't given enough respect to the slot machine and its entertainment value for the slot player in this book, I've made amends by writing a monster chapter for you in *More Frugal Gambling*. I titled it "Not Your Grandma's Slots Anymore" and I thoroughly cover the exciting new world that awaits the slot player in the 21st century. I provide lots of hints to help you choose the machines that match your goals and preferences and give you hints on how to make your gambling bankroll last longer.

Slot Players Rejoice

Slot machines are still almost always negative-expectation games, but all is not lost. You might actually be able to survive if you incorporate the advice in some of the other chapters in this book. Belonging to a slot club, for example, is *mandatory*. Some slot clubs have as much as a 1% cash rebate, which can ease the pain (somewhat) of a 3%-5% house advantage. You can also make up some losses by: getting your fair share of food comps (and eating a lot!); asking your friends to share in the cost of the room to get the most out of your room comps; and tracking down and participating in every promotion with a vengeance. It may be hard work, but by using slot clubs, comps, and promotions, you might actually be able to stay afloat playing the "hungry tigers," the nickname the Orientals in Macau have given their slot machines.

4

Video Poker
The Meat and Potatoes

In the first edition of this book, I began this chapter by saying that video poker was our nuts-and-bolts game of choice, the vehicle we rode up to Level 3 of our gambling pyramid. Nothing has changed in the last six years. Video poker is still the king of games for us.

What *has* changed is the video poker world we find in casinos today. Some of the games I mentioned in the earlier edition no longer exist anywhere (at least none that I know about—and if I did, I wouldn't tell anyone!)—e.g., $1 denomination full-pay Deuces Wild, our lucrative game of choice for several years. Even full-pay Deuces machines on the quarter level are slowly disappearing in many casinos throughout Nevada, and they were rarely ever found in any other gambling venue. It's definitely not as easy to find good games as it was when I first wrote about VP six years ago.

However, those facts of casino life are the very reason that the casino visitor who likes to play video poker needs all the help he can get—and that's what I'm going to give you in this chapter. In one way, players have never had it better when it comes to getting good information about video poker. The printed resources are certainly more numerous than when I started playing 14 years ago. And if you can turn on a computer and surf the Internet, the resources are practically unlimited. Because of this, I'm going to make this chapter a kind of get-you-started tool, with a foundation of basic VP information, some where-to-go-next knowledge, and a lot of encouragement and inspiration to help you to go as far as you wish in your study of this fun game.

Video Poker Paytables

Once upon a time about 25-30 years ago, some mathematicians figured out that, unlike slot machines, you could determine the return of a VP machine by its paytable. About 20 years ago, a few writers/authors began reporting their findings and developing strategies that could be used to extract the most value from the available machines. The late Lenny Frome was one of those writers, and he became the most widely read expert on VP in those early days. He was our original video poker guru, and a friendship developed that Brad and I cherished until his untimely death.

At first there were only a few varieties of video poker, so it was pretty easy to find the best game and learn the accurate strategy for it. But within a few years, the machine manufacturers brought out many new games, or different versions of existing games, all with different paytables. Just before Lenny passed away in 1998, he released his newly revised *Winning Strategies for Video Poker*, a book with 60 games. That meant 60 different paytables and 60 different strategies!

Even Lenny would be astonished at the video poker explosion today, with the advent of multi-line, multi-game, and multi-denomination machines. A single machine might give you the choice of a dozen games in a half-dozen denominations, with different paytables for each combination. It might be possible to have a machine that required learning almost 100 different strategies if you wanted to play every game at every denomination available. So it's a real challenge for the video poker student to stay current. Some of these schedules pay back well; others are terrible. Some have easy-to-learn strategies; some are a real bear.

So all video poker games are not created equal. How do you pick a good one? First you must learn to read the machines, just as you did the slots. The thing is, reading machines is much more important in video poker than it is with slots, because you can determine exactly how much every machine will pay you back in the long run. That's the essence of video poker. The casino's edge (or better yet, the casino's lack of an edge) isn't a deep dark secret for those who study.

Every video poker machine displays a paytable. The paytable gives the payouts for the different hands. Since all payout schedules are based on a 52-card deck (or 53 or 54 cards if there are one or two jokers), any computer can easily calculate how many times you will get a royal flush, straight flush, 4-of-a-kind, full house, and so forth. By feeding the payout schedule into a computer, the experts can determine the exact percentage that machine will return. Return rates usually vary from below 90% all the way up to well over 100%.

How can the ordinary player, who probably is neither a mathematician nor a computer wizard, find out what the expected long-term return is for any particular pay schedule? I've included a long list of VP resources in the back of the book where you can find this information. There's hard-copy material, like books and magazines, the kind of resources I used before I broke down and finally bought a computer in 1997. But even if you're just a newbie computer user in cyberspace, there's a wealth of resources for you, including software and Internet sites.

Video Poker Strategies

So, let's say you've found a video poker machine with a schedule that pays back more than 100%. This, as you have learned, is called a positive-expectation machine. Are you ready to play this game? The answer is no. You not only need to know the paytable and return percentage for a good game, you also need to know the right strategy to use. It does you little good to find a high-return video poker machine, if you have to play it with a seat-of-your-pants guessing strategy.

Don't assume because you've been playing poker around your kitchen table for 25 years that you automatically know how to play video poker correctly; live poker and video poker are two different animals. Actually, your knowledge of live poker can hinder your video poker playing. On the machine, you're not playing against other players; you're playing against a particular pay schedule. And not only is it different from playing in a live game, it's also imperative that you use the proper strategy for the particular variation that you're playing. Things change from schedule to schedule.

I'll give you a simple example. You've probably been taught that you should never draw to an inside straight in draw poker. On many video poker games, that advice holds up. But on some video poker games, it's the right play to draw to an inside straight. There's no way for you to have an accurate feel for this and know intuitively which way to go. Scads of similar rules vary from machine to machine, as well as from live poker strategy.

Again, you might wonder where you can find the correct strategy for each game. And again, refer to the VP Resource List in the back of the book for hard-copy material—books, magazines, and laminated strategy charts—by the experts. However, this will put some limits on you, since new games are popping up so quickly that the hard-copy resources have a hard time staying up to date. Here's the place where the computer user with online access will find it much easier and faster to learn proper strategies, with numerous resources available to help him, including software tutors for practicing at home with no money at risk and for generating strategy charts that you can take to the casino to help you play almost any game skillfully.

A Closer Look at Positive Expectation

What do I mean when I refer to an "over-100% machine?" An over-100% machine simply means a machine that pays back more than you put in. Fantastic, except for one thing: this is factored over a long period of time. It does not mean "over 100% in every session." In fact, an over-100% machine isn't guaranteed to earn you a profit even over what most would consider a long period of time. And it's certainly not graphed by a steady upward curve. The only sure thing I've ever found in gambling is streakiness, and video poker results can be as streaky as it gets.

Also—and this is a very important concept to grasp—the total expected return of a VP game includes getting the expected (by the math) number of royals. A royal contributes approximately 1.7%-2% (depending on the game) to the total payback percentage, and *on average*, royals are hit only about once every 35,000-

45,000 hands (again depending on the game). This is about 80 hours of play at a medium speed.

The problem is that royals don't come right "on schedule." You might get several in a short time (that's no problem!), but you might go several (even many) cycles without one.

So a large majority of royal-less sessions will be losing ones. Why? Because even on a positive-expectation game, you're playing well below 100% during the time you don't hit a royal. This is the reason VP players (indeed all advantage players in any game) must have an adequate bankroll and extra patience. Math expectations take a very long time to reach their full realization; the expected value (EV) given for each VP game assumes an infinite period of play. However, don't let that cause you to give up. The longer you play a positive game, the closer you'll come to a positive result. And the bigger the advantage you can find on a play, the quicker you will get to that positive bottom line.

Playing "full-pay" Deuces Wild (see Chart 3, pg. 52) with computer-perfect ("optimal") strategy, the return percentage is 100.76%. Another way to say this is: for every $100 you put into a full-pay Deuces Wild video poker machine, you'll have a long-term expectation of $100.76. It may look "skinny," but that's a pretty good edge. Unfortunately, only a computer can play computer-perfect strategy. Humans make mistakes. They get tired of sitting and staring at a screen. They get a little fuzzy from the free drinks. The guys get distracted by short skirts on cocktail waitresses. I figure skilled human strategy on a full-pay Deuces Wild machine is more like 100.5%. In these examples, my numbers are based on that one-half-percentage-point advantage.

Playing 25¢ full-pay Deuces, you're making $1.25 bets (five quarters). If you play slowly (say 320 hands per hour), you'll put about $400 through the Deuces

Wild machine in 60 minutes. At our skilled human capability of 100.5%, over that hour your expected theoretical return is $402 (1.005 X $400 = $402). Thus, your expected average return (or win) is $2 per hour. Don't quit your day job!

A Closer Look at Negative Expectation

The flip side of positive expectation is, logically enough, negative expectation. An "under-100% machine" is a machine that pays back less than you put in. Let's say you find a 25¢ Deuces Wild machine that has only one change in the paytable from the full-pay Deuces schedule. A key change—it pays only four coins for 4-of-a-kind instead of five (see Chart 4, pg. 53). That's just one tiny alteration, but it gives the house a whopping 5.7% edge. This means that you're playing a game that returns only 94.3% long-term. Now if you play a slow 320 hands per hour, you're losing an average of $22.80 per hour (.057 X $400)—and that's on a 25¢ machine.

Does the $2-per-hour profit from full-pay Deuces look better to you now? And does the $22.80-per-hour loss convince you to read paytables carefully? One of the main reasons for all the new video poker variations is that casinos know there are a lot of players with a little bit of video poker knowledge. Many people now know that full-pay Jacks or Better and Deuces Wild are good games, but they're not real careful about reading the paytables to make sure that full-pay is what they're playing. Point them toward any Jacks or Better or Deuces machine and they assume it pays liberally. The casinos, of course, make sure that they aren't: "Play this game. It's almost like the other one that pays a lot more."

This occasionally backfires on a casino when it

monkeys with a pay schedule of a well-known machine and the changes result in a larger payback percentage. If you become a true student of the game, you'll be able to spot these situations, know what changes to make in the strategy, and take advantage to make a lot of money on these machines, until the casino wises up and fixes the schedule or removes the machines entirely.

Jacks or Better

Jacks or Better is the basic video poker game. One of the first to come out, it's considered something of a video poker standard. The full-pay version is known as 9/6 Jacks or Better, meaning the payback (with one coin in) for a full house is 9 coins and for a flush is 6 coins. Full-pay Jacks or Better has a long-term return percentage of 99.5%. It's not a positive game; as we've seen, the casino has a .5% advantage. But because it's often available in many venues, in many denominations from quarters up — and because a number of other video poker variations are derived from it — I also consider it the best game for beginners. The strategy is one of the easiest to learn, because it's more intuitive than many others. It has also become the game for many experienced players, especially high rollers, because it's sometimes offered in luxurious casinos where a high level of comps is available. And on any level, you can often get enough cashback from the slot club or from a promotion to make it an over-100% play.

Chart 1 is what the paytable for a 9/6 Jacks or Better video poker machine looks like. Chart 2 is also a Jacks or Better paytable, but with a critical difference: it's an 8/5 machine. Note the difference in the payouts for full house and flush; this lowers the return to 97.3%.

I'm not going to provide you with the strategy, which is readily available in any number of books and computer software programs. See the list of Resources in the back of this book for recommendations. Also, reading my second book, *More Frugal Gambling*, is the best next step for the student of video poker. It has a very long chapter on VP that's full of specific details to help choose games and learn strategies.

Chart 1 — Jacks or Better
25¢ • 9/6 • 5-Coin Maximum

	1st Coin	2nd Coin	3rd Coin	4th Coin	5th Coin
Royal Flush	250	500	750	1000	4000
Straight Flush	50	100	150	200	250
4-of-a-Kind	25	50	75	100	125
Full House	9	18	27	36	45
Flush	6	12	18	24	30
Straight	4	8	12	16	20
3-of-a-Kind	3	6	9	12	15
Two Pair	2	4	6	8	10
Jacks or Better	1	2	3	4	5

Payback: 99.5%

Chart 2 — Jacks or Better
25¢ • 8/5 • 5-Coin Maximum

	1st Coin	2nd Coin	3rd Coin	4th Coin	5th Coin
Royal Flush	250	500	750	1000	4000
Straight Flush	50	100	150	200	250
4-of-a-Kind	25	50	75	100	125
Full House	8	16	24	32	40
Flush	5	10	15	20	25
Straight	4	8	12	16	20
3-of-a-Kind	3	6	9	12	15
Two Pair	2	4	6	8	10
Jacks or Better	1	2	3	4	5

Payback: 97.3%

Deuces Wild

Our favorite quarter video poker game for many years was full-pay Deuces Wild (see Chart 3 for the full-pay payout schedule). Full-pay Deuces is an over-100% game and, for many low-roller advantage players, this is where the money is. Most people learn how to play video poker on 9/6 machines, and we were no exception. But once we tried Deuces Wild, we were hooked.

In Deuces Wild, you have to pay close attention to the pay schedules, since a seemingly slight change can have a pronounced effect on the return percentage. Examine the two Deuces Wild pay schedules that follow. The first schedule is the full-pay version. It's sometimes referred to as a 25/15/9/5 schedule, reflecting the number of coins returned for a wild royal, 5-of-a-kind, straight flush, and 4-of-a-kind (with one coin played).

Chart 3 — Full-Pay Deuces Wild (FPDW)
25¢ • 5-Coin Maximum

	1st Coin	2nd Coin	3rd Coin	4th Coin	5th Coin
Royal Flush	250	500	750	1000	4000
Four Deuces	200	400	600	800	1000
Wild Royal	25	50	75	100	125
5-of-a-Kind	15	30	45	60	75
Straight Flush	9	18	27	36	45
4-of-a-Kind	(5)	10	15	20	25
Full House	3	6	9	12	15
Flush	2	4	6	8	10
Straight	2	4	6	8	10
3-of-a-Kind	1	2	2	4	5

Payback: 100.7%

The most important entry is the one for 4-of-a-kind. Again, notice the difference in return when just this one payout is lowered by a single coin.

	1st Coin	2nd Coin	3rd Coin	4th Coin	5th Coin
Chart 4 — Short-Pay Deuces Wild *25¢ • 5-Coin Maximum*					
Royal Flush	250	500	750	1000	4000
Four Deuces	200	400	600	800	1000
Wild Royal	25	50	75	100	125
5-of-a-Kind	15	30	45	60	75
Straight Flush	9	18	27	36	45
4-of-a-Kind	(4)	8	12	16	20
Full House	3	6	9	12	15
Flush	2	4	6	8	10
Straight	2	4	6	8	10
3-of-a-Kind	1	2	2	4	5
Payback: 94.3%					

The importance of playing the good Deuces Wild pay schedules should be clear. But it's not only about the positive expectation. The wild-card factor produces a particular kind of thrill. When that wild card comes up in the first five cards, there's no telling how good the hand that's in store for you will be. For many players, Deuces Wild has more psychological attraction than any other video poker game.

Another aspect of Deuces Wild we like is that you don't have to hit a royal flush to have a winning session. Deuces Wild comes with a mini-jackpot. Roughly every 5,000 hands on average you'll hit four deuces, which pays $250 (on the quarter machines with max coins played). Getting a four-deuce hand can give you a winning session without hitting the great big royal flush.

Another reason I like Deuces Wild is that the strategy is simple to learn and easy to remember. Some people disagree and think that the strategy for Jacks or Better is easier, but Brad and I have always thought otherwise. The strategy is easy because it's broken down by how many deuces you have. Organizationally, instead of one long chart, you have several little charts. For me, that makes all the difference.

There is one disadvantage to Deuces. It's a more volatile game, which produces much bigger swings between winning and losing sessions than Jacks or Better does. You can rack up many many losing sessions in a row. If you don't hit a mini-jackpot (four deuces) or a royal, you're usually guaranteed to be a loser that session.

When Full-Pay is Not Full-Pay

Another common question that people ask me is, "Why would casinos offer machines that pay more than 100%? Don't the casinos have to have an edge on every game? How are they going to pay for all the lights?" (It's amazing how concerned people are about the casinos' ability to pay their light bills.)

The fact is, the casinos make healthy profits on machines that have the potential to pay back over 100%. How is that possible? Two reasons. First, the 100% payback is for max-coin play only (the bonus for a max-coin royal flush is worth about 1.2%). Secondly, the positive payout assumes the players employ a perfect playing strategy. As I've pointed out, most players understand a little about video poker paytables, but accurate play takes some study.

I've seen full-pay Deuces Wild machines in more than one casino with signs that say, "This machine pays back 98%." Now, I know that full-pay Deuces can return 100.76%, so why are they advertising it as paying back 98%? Here's why. The casino knows that in the past, when it's tallied all its wins and losses from that machine, the bottom line has been a profit of 2%. This is due to sub-optimal and short-coin play (remember, when you play less than the maximum coins, you don't qualify for the big royal flush bonus). Very few play at a positive level, so the casino wins its 2% — or more.

A lot of 100%+ video poker machines — Double Bonus games, for example — have such non-intuitive (even bizarre) strategies that if you don't know and abide by them, you could be playing at a 95%-return level. You'd sometimes be better off playing slot machines!

"How Much Money Will I Need?"

This is another common question we're asked, though a lot of people just assume we can do what we do in the casinos because we have all the money in the world, which we don't! Everyone wants to know how much money is necessary to allow the long-term percentages to bear out. For a long time, a general rule for a positive game held that you should have a bankroll equal to three royal flushes — usually $3,000 for a quarter game — so you wouldn't go broke before you reached that long-term profit expectation. And our own experience the first six years while we played at the quarter level seemed to confirm this figure. Brad and I together played quarter FPDW three to eight hours a day, at least 100 days a year, and we never needed a "bankroll" (the amount of actual money we have to gamble with) greater than $3,000. In other words, our longest losing streak playing 25¢ machines never resulted in cumulative losses greater than $3,000.

The one time that we came close to accumulating losses of $3,000 was the most inopportune time of all for Lady Luck to leave us. It was the week the "48 Hours" video crew was following us around. We were bragging to them about how well we did in Vegas playing video poker, and here we were losing consistently, nearly reaching the $3,000 loss point.

Fortunately, at the end of the week, we won a car, which catapulted us back into the black and saved us some public embarrassment. However, it scared us enough that from that time forward, we upped our bankroll requirement to $5,000. After that, if we ever started approaching $3,000 in losses, we didn't get as nervous; we had that extra $2,000 to keep us from seeing the bottom of the bankroll barrel. We never had to touch that extra reserve, but it gave us a secure feeling when we were in the midst of a long dry spell.

An important note here: Success in gambling is never 100% guaranteed. That's why I always insist that you never gamble with money you can't afford to lose. On the other hand, there are many things you can do to reduce your ROR (risk of ruin), meaning your chance of going broke. The reason we never needed more than $3,000 was that: 1) We always played positive games that gave us a big edge; 2) we played very accurate strategy; and 3) most of all, we made heavy use of the benefits of the slot club system, especially cashback. We also chased promotions tirelessly, looking for multi-point days and extra bonuses.

Players who neglect any of these areas will need a much bigger bankroll. And they increase their chances of going broke sooner or later. If you play negative-expectation VP games with few or no slot club benefits or bonuses, you're pretty much *guaranteed* to lose. Maybe you'll win one day, or one week, or even for a longer stretch. But just as the sun rises in the east, you *will* lose over the long term, and usually sooner than later.

If you have a partner and the two of you are playing on one bankroll, you don't need twice as much. You need the same $3,000-$5,000 for quarter machines as if only one of you is playing. Think of it this way: would you need more money if you were playing eight hours a day by yourself than if two of you each played four hours a day? No. In fact, partnership play smoothes out the ups and downs a little.

"Well, I don't have $3,000 to lose," you might say. Neither do we! I mean, we have it, but we certainly don't want to lose it. This $3,000 bankroll that I've been talking about is not $3,000 that we intend to part with permanently. We like to think that we sometimes loan back our gambling bankroll to the casinos while our play is "averaging itself out."

Let's say we're starting from scratch. You and I have studied to play video poker expertly and we're launching our low-roller careers with $3,000 cash playing only positive-expectation games. Now, we might start off losing $1,000 while we wait to hit the royal flush. And then maybe we hit a $1,000 royal and get back up to our $3,000.

Then maybe we get lucky and hit two more royals within a couple of hours. So now we've built our bankroll up to $5,000. This doesn't mean we take out $2,000 and spend it. We keep it in our bankroll temporarily (we like to have a $5,000 bankroll anyway), and it sees us through subsequent stretches when we don't hit a royal. If the big drought results in a $3,000 loss, we'll be back down to a bankroll of $2,000 again. But eventually we'll hit another royal.

The ebb and flow of winning and losing goes on and on. But the way we do it, putting in lots of hours on only positive-expectation games, and combining with slot club rebates and promotional opportunities, we are fairly well protected against ever losing the whole original $3,000 permanently.

About the slot club and promotional returns just alluded to, this is where much of our profit (and our reserve in case of a temporary poor run of cards) comes from. When you take a 100%+ machine and add in strong slot club benefits and promotions so you're playing at *well* over 100%, the profits will come sooner or later. We like to play a good enough pay schedule, combined with a good enough slot club and a good enough promotion, so that if we never hit the royal, we'll still break even. When that's accomplished, the royal flushes represent pure profit (read the next two chapters to see how this works). Although there is never a guarantee, when you're always playing at well over 100% you have a good chance of making a profit if you can play long enough. At some point (though I can't tell you exactly when), you'll be able to take that profit out of your bankroll. Spend it, put it in the bank, invest it. You've earned it.

Changing Machines

One thing that many people agonize over is when they should change machines. The answer is that if you're playing the same paytable, it doesn't really matter. But it's amazing how many people refuse to believe it. The math, remember, is based on play over the long term. The averages say that you'll get one royal about every 40,000 hands. So it's all the same whether you play 40,000 hands on one machine or 1,000 hands on 40 different machines or 100 hands on 400 machines.

Of course, in real life you could get no royals in 80,000 hands or five royals in 20,000 hands. Still, it makes no difference how many machines it takes you to do it.

Do I ever change machines? Sure I change machines. I change machines if the seat's not comfortable, or the buttons are sticking, or the air-conditioning is blowing cold air on my neck, or the person playing next to me is a grouch or a smoker. And I don't mind admitting it, but I occasionally change machines just because I'm disgusted with the one I'm playing, when it hasn't given me anything good for a long while. Again, it doesn't have anything to do with the math. It's just that losing is getting me psyched out and I want to walk around, clear my head, and start fresh in a different part of the casino.

Go ahead: Hop from one machine to another. But as you do, remember that it's for a psychological feeling, not for a mathematical reason.

A Royal Flush Story

I once went to a casino specifically to play a good dollar machine on a double-points day for the slot club. There was only one vacant machine, and a change girl told me that someone had hit a $4,000 royal on it earlier that day. Most people probably wouldn't sit down at that machine, since it had already given up a royal. I knew, however, that mathematically the first royal didn't make any difference. I sat down without giving it a second thought.

I started playing at 5 in the evening. At 9:45 I hit a $4,000 royal. After being paid, I stayed right where I was and kept playing. Now, you might think that I was pressing my luck, that I should have left that machine then. I only had about $600 in it, and I'd taken $4,000 out of it. And, the machine had now paid out two royals in one day. But I said, "No. It's still double-point day and I want to keep playing."

At about 11:15 I hit another $4,000 royal. Now the machine had paid out $12,000 in royals (that I knew of) that day. By no stretch of the imagination had $12,000 been won back by the machine. I'd played it half the day and lost back less than $1,000.

So there I was, $7,000 ahead and waiting to collect my second $4,000 when a man started talking to me. He patted me on my shoulder and said, "Honey, lemme give you a little advice here. You've got to quit right now and take that money home, because if you stay here you'll lose it all and more."

I patted *him* on the shoulder and said, "Well sir, I don't know what you play, but I'll tell you something that I don't tell just anybody. I'm playing a positive-expectation game that pays back over 100%, so the longer I play, the more likely it is that I'm going to win more."

Although it might be wise for many people to stop playing for a while so they can celebrate their big win, most players recite a myth for their reason for quitting. They have a very difficult time understanding or believing that there is no such thing as a machine being "played out." In other words, even though someone hit a royal on a particular machine earlier in the day (or week or month), it doesn't mean that the machine won't give up another royal for some predetermined amount of time. By the same token, there's also no such thing as a "due factor." If a machine hasn't paid a royal for weeks, it becomes no more likely to hit than at any other time.

I left at the stroke of midnight. Had there been more time left to accumulate double points, I'd have continued to play for as long as I could stay alert.

Deviating from Optimal Strategy

People ask me if, on occasion, I ignore the strict rules of video poker's optimal strategy. They want to know if I sometimes have a feeling or a hunch that something's going to happen, and whether or not I act on it. My answer is "NO, NO, NEVER." If you don't trust the strategy charts, which have been derived by mathematicians and computer scientists, then there's not much hope for you.

As I've mentioned, I'm not a math expert myself. But I trust that the computer experts who write these books have worked out the statistics, and other computer experts have checked them twice. If the Deuces Wild strategy chart tells me to draw to an inside straight, which goes against everything I've ever learned about playing regular poker, then I go for that inside straight with all the gusto I can muster! Trust me, the computer has determined that you will win more often by going for that straight than you will if you don't.

Think about it. When you buy a video poker resource, most of them running anywhere from $5 for a strategy card to $40 for software, you're purchasing the results of thousands of dollars worth of research conducted by high-priced experts. If you've ever played VP, even sparingly, you know you can feed $100 into a machine and lose it in a matter of minutes. Investing in good resources will bring better returns!

And there's another benefit to playing "by the book." Employing accurate strategy is actually comforting. It cushions the blow when you lose. And you will lose. No one wins every session. In fact, even expert players lose more sessions than they win. But when you're in a losing session, or even in the middle of a series of them, it's comforting to know that the math is correct. You can say, "I may be losing now, but I know that I'm making the right plays, I have an edge, and eventually I'll come out ahead."

If you're playing one way one time because you feel like it (such as playing recklessly for the elusive royal) and playing another way another time because you feel differently (shooting for four aces), then you're never entitled to that comforting feeling. You're just being tossed around like a little rowboat in the ocean of hunches and luck, because you have no anchor. A computer-generated strategy is your anchor. You hang onto it when you play to help you weather the storms of chance.

You hang onto it especially tight when you're losing. When you're winning you don't need an anchor (or a security blanket or a teddy bear). When you're losing, though, you need all the buttressing and bucking up you can get.

What Denomination?

You may remember from the Introduction that we started out as bona fide high rollers, betting $25, $50, up to $100 dollars a hand at the blackjack tables. Then we descended all the way down to quarter video poker machines, where we stayed for five years before we started moving up to dollar video poker.

There are several reasons for our move back up. One is that we now have a bigger bankroll, thanks to our winnings at the quarter level. And when we were staying in hotels, it helped us get the comps we needed at their casinos more quickly, allowing us also to work promotions at other casinos. Plus, many promotions are much more lucrative if you can play them at the dollar level. Some of the promotions are set up in such a way that you can hardly complete them playing quarters; you can do it in four hours playing at a dollar machine, but you'd have to put in 16 hours at a quarter machine.

People ask us how we can play at high denominations and still drop back to lower denoms at times. "Don't you lose some of the thrill?" This *is* the biggest danger of moving up: some people can never drop down again. It depends on your personality and "excitement level." Since I'm busy writing so much of the time, I don't have many hours for the VP machines, so I do find that I prefer the excitement of higher denominations. On the other hand, Brad has more leisure time, so when he plays alone, he often plays quarter FPDW, which he can do indefinitely and never get bored.

People ask us if we're no longer low rollers, since we can often be found at the dollar Triple or Five Play machines and sometimes even playing a machine that takes as much as $50 per hand. I guess we don't really fit one label, since we move all over the various denominations. What it really comes down to is that we play the denomination that fits our goals for that day, within the range we can afford, which is within our bankroll. We try to play with the best advantage we can, depending on the time element. Now that we're getting older, we don't have the stamina we once did to play that many hours in one day. So we look for good promotions that will allow our two- or three-hour playing limit to produce the most benefits.

You might ordinarily play quarters at one casino, but go to dollars on bonus-point days. You might play higher when you're staying in a luxury hotel-casino, so you'll earn higher-level comps, then drop down in denomination when it doesn't take as much play to earn the basic comps in a mid-level casino.

But there's one *big* problem with switching around denominations: It will make your VP results *much* more choppy. We've had long periods when we were winning on the lower levels, but losing on the higher ones. Eventually, we play enough at each level to achieve the long-term results we want. But in the meantime, the roller-coaster ride is hair-raising and frustrating—and many people just can't stand the emotional ups-and-downs.

There's also another big danger for people who want to go up in denomination. Many more machines on the quarter level have positive-payback schedules than on dollars and up. Most players don't realize how much bigger a bankroll they'll need. You don't just need four times the bankroll to move from quarters to dollars as you would if you were moving to the same game. You may have to move to a game that gives you a much smaller edge, and depending on the reduction in edge, you might need $10,000-$40,000 more to give yourself a good chance of not going broke.

The introduction of the more exciting multi-line games has been the ruin of many players who underestimated their bankroll needs. These machines usually have lower pay schedules. Former single-line quarter players who go to quarter Triple Play often don't realize how much faster their money can disappear even if they're playing the same pay schedule. And if the payoff has been reduced, the increased drain on their bankroll is a shocking experience. Then, even if they drop down to nickel Five Play, they almost always have to play an inferior pay schedule that gives them no edge at all, so they lose the hope of a long-term positive expectation as well as still losing their money faster than on their original good-payback single-line machine.

The Payoff

Although there are a few other ways to get to the top of Level 3 (by mastering other positive-expectation casino games like blackjack or live poker), the easiest for the average serious gambler is video poker. Actually, "easy" may be a poor choice of words. Not everyone can or wants to do it. It does take intense desire and conscientious study. But you're well rewarded for your efforts. You might not only get to the top of Level 3, but with determination you might be able to knock on the door of Level 4. The next three chapters show you how to use slot clubs, the comp system, and promotions to accelerate your rise to the top.

5

Slot Clubs
Join Or Else

Editor's Note: Slot club (and promotion) particulars are in a constant state of flux, and many that are covered here have come, gone, and/or changed. The coverage in these chapters is meant to provide a general understanding of the strategies.

This chapter is for every gambler, no matter what casino game you play. Slot clubs were invented for machine players, but more and more casinos are hooking their table games into the same system. The most powerful weapon in your war against the mighty casinos is a little seven-square-inch piece of plastic that the casinos give you for free: the slot club card. It looks like a credit card, but with a wonderful difference: *It pays you*. Playing *any* machine in a casino without using a slot club card is like going up to your hotel room after each gambling session and throwing a fistful of dollars out the window.

If you've mastered the strategies for the over-100%-payback video poker games, you're already solidly on

Level 3 of our gambling pyramid. Adding slot club benefits will take you higher, perhaps even up to that exclusive tip of the triangle. If you're not quite so discriminating and your game choices include less-than-100% payback options, your slot club membership can reduce your losses and perhaps even put you into breakeven or positive territory.

For most of you, joining slot clubs will be the best way to climb out of the despair of Level 1 up to the satisfaction of Level 2, where you'll begin to notice your losses getting smaller. Using slot club benefits is a must for all casual slot and video poker players; it's the only way to keep the negative-expectation games from eating you alive.

The Basics

Slot clubs are complicated, and understanding their inner workings and all the tricks that the knowledgeable players employ to take advantage of them is a never-ending study for the serious gambler. In *More Frugal Gambling*, I go into great detail about exploiting the club systems, promotions, and benefits. In this chapter, my aim is to provide the basic building blocks for your foray into the world of slot clubs.

If you've never joined a slot club, here's how to go about it.

First, you have to find the slot club booth. If you're energetic, wander around the casino until you see a manned counter with a big sign saying something like "Connection Card" or "Cash Club" or "VIP Club" or "One Card." If you don't want to meander and prefer to march right up to the booth, simply ask a casino employee where to find the slot club.

Once there, look around for an application form; they're usually sitting out in a plastic holder. Fill one out, truthfully (though on most, providing your Social Security number and other private information is optional), then wait your turn and hand it, along with your valid identification (which is now required everywhere to join), to the next available booth attendant, who'll input the information into the system and hand you your credit-card-size slot card. That's all there is to it.

Then insert your card into the card reader of any slot or video gambling machine that you play. That's how you start earning points. Be sure to pay attention to the digital read-out on the tiny screen next to the card slot. You're looking for it to read, "Hello [your name]," or "Welcome" or "Card Accepted." If it reads "Unable to Read" or "Please Reinsert Card," keep trying until your card is accepted. If you don't, you'll lose any points you might have earned during that session.

Periodically, return to the slot club booth, hand the attendant your card, and ask what comps, or cashback, or both, you're entitled to. If that's all you do—and never give another thought to the slot club—you'll still outdistance everyone who doesn't get even that far. You'll be earning and collecting comps and/or cashback for your play, which puts you way ahead in the gambling game. And, just as important, you'll get into the casino database, which means you'll start seeing the miracle of casino mail, which can bring unbelievable comps and other benefits.

If you want to kick up your knowledge of slot clubs another notch or two, there's much more you can do. Definitely read the slot club brochure. It should explain whether you can earn cashback or comps or both; each casino has its own system. Often, it delineates how much points are worth: how much play is required to earn a point and how many points you need for comps and/or cashback.

For example, it might say, "$1 of coin-in gives you one slot club point." So, if you're playing a $1 machine with a five-coin maximum bet, you now know that for every hand you play you earn 5 points. If this is a club that gives cash for points, the brochure should also say how many points equal $1 in cashback. If it's a comp-only club, it should have a "menu" listing how many points you need to eat at various restaurants and redeem for other benefits. So now you can calculate how much money you'll have to play through the machine to earn what you want.

Unfortunately, not all casinos put all the information you need in their brochures. So your next step is to ask specific questions at the booth. And sometimes the math is a complicated puzzle. One resource to help you here is the *Frugal Video Poker* software I talked about in the last chapter and have included in the resource section at the back of the book. It has a very useful feature, no matter whether you play VP or slot machines, that helps you figure slot club benefits.

After you've played enough to get the required points for what you want, return to the slot club booth. You'll have to hand over your card and a photo ID. The attendant will hand back a slip of paper that you take to the restaurant (if it's a food comp you've requested) or to the cashier's cage (if it's cashback you want).

Those are the basics for sizing up and using a slot club. Everything else—covered in this chapter and in the big slot club chapter in *More Frugal Gambling*—is nuance and fine-tuning. Still, the more you know about slot clubs, the more your gambling experience is enhanced. That's why between the two books, you'll find nearly 70 pages on slot clubs.

Choosing Your First Slot Club
Different clubs for different rubs!

The requirements of a slot club in the view of an expert video poker player who's out to make a profit in Las Vegas casinos will be very different from a vacationing slot player who gets his biggest kick out of getting his hotel rooms for free in Atlantic City. A local slot player who never needs rooms but hates to cook might look for a slot club that offers the highest payback in food credits, while a video poker player who can only visit a gambling destination during the busiest times of year might try to find a slot club that's best at providing special handling for room, restaurant, and show reservations. After a while, you'll become adept at sizing up slot clubs for what they offer in relation to what you want. But for starters, my advice is to join the slot club at your favorite casino.

When I say your favorite casino, I assume that you're being realistic. You can't expect to waltz into a fancy Las Vegas Strip casino with $40 in quarters and get the world handed to you on a platter. If your goal is to play enough 25¢ video poker to get food and room comps, you'll need to join the slot clubs at the mid-range or second-tier casinos. These aren't the most luxurious resorts, but they do have slot clubs that award good cash rebates and/or offer generous room and food comps for low-roller play.

The Stardust's slot club, you may recall, launched Brad and me on our path in 1990. After we discovered video poker, we found that the Stardust had many of the machines that we wanted to play. Soon we learned that the slot club paid cashback for play. Joining was a no-brainer. In fact, if cash rebates had been the only thing we got from the slot club, we would have been satisfied. Actually, in the beginning we thought that cashback was all we were entitled to. Our big surprise came after we returned home and started getting fabulous offers in the mail, things like coupons for free buffets, vouchers to stay three or four nights free, and invitations to attend shows and special parties. Most of these offers had monetary value. And while the rest of the benefits didn't save or earn us money, they made our Vegas experiences more enjoyable. That was, and still is, important to us.

Becoming a regular customer at the Stardust served us well in our early low-roller days. I recommend you follow a similar strategy of selecting one favorite casino and putting enough points on its slot club card to become an established member. I call this primary selection the "core club."

The number of points needed to achieve regular club status is different at every casino. The Stardust started giving us comps early on; that will happen at many other casinos, too. Some places will absolutely shock you. We've joined slot clubs where we put no more than a single roll of quarters through a machine and the first mail we got from that casino was an offer for three free nights. Usually, though, there's some required point level that you have to reach.

Some casinos have a tiered membership structure—the longer you play, the more the casino will reward you, upgrading your comps at each level. Some will actually increase your cash-back percentage after a specified lifetime point total is achieved.

According to slot club specialist Jeffrey Compton, activation levels are dropping slowly as competition gets more intense.

The Buddy System

It used to be that you could earn comps faster if two of you played on one person's card, thus earning points at double the usual rate. But it's a little dicier these days. Casinos now discourage two people from playing on one person's card. In fact, if you're playing a promotion where the rule is you must have your card inserted, you'd better have your own card inserted; otherwise the casino is within its rights to withhold any winnings.

I recommend using the buddy system only if two people share the same address, the same last name, the same bankroll, or any combination thereof. There's nothing unethical about a couple that's married or lives together having one slot club account per casino.

A slight variation on this theme is to start out with a single account, then add a second account in the other partner's name later. Using this strategy, one of you signs up for the slot club and gets two cards in one name initially. Both of you play on the same card for a visit or two, in order to accumulate enough points to get the card activated. On a later trip, the other partner picks up two more cards with a separate membership number. Now you have two cards for each name at one casino.

In our case, Brad got a card at the Stardust first. After we'd put about 1,000 points on it, we got a mailing for three free nights. When we went back to use our free nights, we put 200 points a day on his card to keep it qualified. Then I got two cards in my name and we proceeded to accumulate points on that account. Soon we were getting duplicate invitations. We would stay three days in his name, then three more days in mine.

Of course, we were always careful to stay qualified in each name. We both used the card in my name when the room was in my name, and switched when it was in Brad's. Some casinos still insist that married couples share one account. If you bump into one, gently remind the attendant—and her supervisor, and the supervisor's supervisor, if necessary—that we're now in the 21st century, where many married couples have separate last names, phone numbers, bank accounts, and bankrolls, if they even bothered to get married at all!

Be gentle but insistent until you're given separate accounts. That way you can often earn up to twice the benefits that you would with a single account for both of you.

Adding Core Clubs

When the time comes to branch out to your second casino, you simply employ the same strategy all over again. Now you can stay in Casino A for six days (three in each name), then move to Casino B for six days. All of a sudden you're staying in Las Vegas for 12 days free and you only have to move once. You're starting to flex your low-roller muscles.

Having at least one core casino is such a strong strategy that I recommend you make sure you're well established before splitting your play to earn benefits at another. And keep in mind that you have to maintain a certain amount of play at your core casino (or casinos) to keep the free rooms and special invitations coming. This is called "keeping qualified," and each casino has its own maintenance requirements. If we stayed six nights at the Stardust, then went over to the Riviera for six nights, we played at the Stardust while we stayed there and played at the Riviera while we stayed there. That way, we knew they'd both invite us back for another round of freebies. Some people spread their play around in so many casinos that they never qualify for much at any one of them. Although we belong to more than 100 or so slot clubs around the country, we play regularly only at seven or eight of them. Sometimes we get invitations to participate in something special at a casino where we don't usually stay or play, but on the whole we patronize our regular set of casinos in each gambling venue.

Did you notice that figure of 100 slot clubs above? Those take into account all of our "fringe clubs" (discussed next), and they pay sporadic dividends. In Las Vegas, for example, as many as 20 casinos might send you free-room offers for the slow times of year, particularly December and January. Las Vegas is famous for giving away the store the week before Christmas. That week we can get 20 rooms for ourselves, or one each for 20 of our closest friends. Almost every casino in which you belong to the slot club and have played minimally will give you a free room that week.

But to stay free any time of year, you need to concentrate your play. Playing extra heavy in one or two casinos will help you get comped rooms over Christmas, New Year's Eve, the Super Bowl, and other holiday weekends throughout the year. When the town is full because of a large convention, you'll be able to find a room easier in the casinos where you've played the most.

Fringe Clubs

Prior advice notwithstanding, it never hurts to just join the slot club, even if you never plan to play in that casino. I've received valuable mailings from slot clubs at casinos where I've never put a single quarter into a machine. Right after you join, they might send you one or two mailings before giving up on you. Sometimes they'll court you with a free night (or two or three). Other casinos will keep you on their mailing list forever, even if you don't play. I've been on one casino's list for eight years and I haven't played there yet! They've never given me a free room, but they send a monthly newsletter that sometimes contains coupons for discounted or free food.

When do I join a new slot club? If I walk by a slot club booth where I'm not a member and there is no line, I'll usually sign up. If there's a long line, I usually won't wait, unless I have some time to kill.

Often I'll join a new slot club because it's offering a sign-on bonus of some kind. It could be just a small souvenir — a keychain or a deck of cards — but often it's something more valuable. We've received an expensive logo sports bag, a fanny pack, sports drink cups, a shot glass, a beach towel, and a number of T-shirts. Often the bonus translates into money in our pockets. Some casinos offer double points for play during the first 24 hours after you sign up.

How do you find out about these new-member bonuses? As I'll detail more in the chapter on promotions, you must look everywhere — in the local newspapers, in the freebie tourist magazines, on the casino marquees, on banners near the slot club booth. One time at Caesars in Atlantic City, I picked up a casino newsletter from a rack just inside the entrance and in it was a coupon for a free pull on Megabucks when you joined the slot club. (No, I didn't win the $4.1 million, but I grabbed the free opportunity to go for it.)

Should you refrain from joining new clubs in order to wait for some sort of sign-on bonus? I'd say no; I've found that joining as soon as possible speeds up the chance of getting lucrative offers by mail that tend to be more valuable than the typical sign-on bonus. A possible exception is Atlantic City. The competition there is fierce, especially when it comes to the bused-in day-trippers. These players, many of them senior citizens with time to ferret out the good deals, are savvy consumers. They wait until a juicy promotion comes up before they join. And juicy many of them are. In November 1996, Harrah's offered new members up to a $250 reimbursement for losses during their first hour of play. Wow! That was the best sign-on bonus I'd ever seen, up till that point. Since then, I've seen others in Atlantic City that were good for more than $1,000.

Knowing Where You Stand

At some casinos, the printed literature, which explains how the club operates and what points are worth, is very clear. One casino in Las Vegas, for example, used to be a good example of a slot club that gave you all the information up front. They told you that as soon as you earned 1,000 points, you were entitled to two free nights every month on a Tuesday, Wednesday, or Thursday. When you reached 2,000 points, you could stay on a Sunday and Monday as well. At 20,000 points, you could stay any night of the year, even holidays, and at 50,000 points, you were entitled to a suite. They also told you that to keep qualified, you had to put at least 300 points on your card per free day. All that was very clear. You knew that if you earned the 600 points during your two free days, you could stay there again for free the next time. If you didn't, you had to pay.

Most casinos aren't nearly as straightforward as that casino used to be. It's often hard to determine just how much you have to play to stay on the comp list. This is inconvenient, but it's not always bad. It actually works both ways. Some slot clubs have dropped us from the mailing list after only half a year of not playing there. Others keep sending us offers for free nights even though we never play there. One couple I know has stayed two or three nights free every month for two years at one casino and never spent a nickel keeping qualified. Of course, most casinos aren't that generous. And, for me, there's a loyalty issue here. By my way of thinking, it isn't right to stay for free and not play. If a casino gives me my free days, I'll give them some play in return. The only exception is if we get to the casino and they've taken out all the high-return machines we were expecting to play. Then we won't play there; we don't play bad machines for comps of any kind. But we also won't plan on staying there for free again.

How much play you need in order to know where you stand varies. And that's something you can only learn by doing. We used to play a lot at one casino, until they took out most of their high-return video poker machines. Now, instead of the free-room offers they used to send us, our invitations are for low-priced rooms. This casino has a slot club that isn't forthcoming with the important information about point-redemption requirements, so the only thing I know for sure is that we're below the free-room level.

Sometimes you can get the information you need about different levels of status by asking at the slot club booth, or even by calling up and talking to casino marketing. But in most cases they just won't tell you. They act as though it's some big corporate secret. Jeffrey Compton calls these "don't ask, won't tell" systems. I prefer the casinos that keep you informed right up front, and thankfully, many casinos are heading in that direction.

Because we always have separate memberships, Brad and I sometimes get inadvertent clues about secret rating systems. During a visit, one of us may put a lot more points on a particular casino's slot club card than the other, which results in our receiving two different promotions in the mail. One of us gets an offer for four free nights and the other gets an invitation for three. One gets 50 tickets for a drawing while the other gets only 10. One gets $50 credit at the logo shop while the other gets $20.

Other variables factor into determining what you get. Some casinos seem to send out blanket promotions to everyone. Others vary their promotions according to how many points you have, how long you've been a member, what denomination machine you play, where you live, how old you are, and whether you play slots or video poker. Lots of clubs have higher comp standards for quarter players than dollar players. Many slot clubs in the recent past didn't award slot club credits for nickel play, but that's changing fast, now that nickel and even penny machines are becoming so popular.

A few casinos don't differentiate between slot and video poker players, but most do. You often have to play twice the amount through a video poker machine as you do through a slot machine to get the same number of points. Most casinos give their slot players much better benefits than they do their video poker players. Why? Because the casinos know that the slot player will probably lose more money. (This difference in slot club payoff might motivate slot players to switch to video poker—even the casinos are telling you that video poker players lose less.)

Cashback from Machine Play

Do you recall the example I gave in the video poker chapter illustrating that even if you play quarter full-pay Deuces Wild slowly, you can earn a $2-per-hour profit? Let's expand on that idea. But first, you need to understand that there's a difference between the money you put *into* a machine and the money you put *through* a machine. Here's the difference. Let's say you play one roll of quarters; that means you've put $10 *into* the machine. Maybe you hit a couple of 3-of-a-kinds, a flush, and a full house and you now have 65 credits. You wouldn't go buy another roll of quarters, would you? No, you'd play off the credits. As you do, you're putting more money *through* the machine. It doesn't matter whether you drop an actual quarter into the machine or use one credit, you are still putting 25¢ through. You could conceivably put $10 into the machine and play $400 through it if you were hitting well and the credits kept building up.

Say Casino A gives you back $1 in cash for every $400 you play through its machines. That calculates out to one-quarter of one percent (.25%) that Casino A will rebate you on your video poker action. That's on top of your .5% profit for playing the positive machine. So now you're earning .75% profit and you're no longer making $2 an hour, you're making $3 per hour ($2 from the machine and $1 from the slot club).

Now, consider a slot club that pays a .5% cash rebate. Let's do the arithmetic for a double-point day on a 9/6 $1 Jacks or Better machine that returns 99.5%. If you play very fast and use the bill feed, you can get in 600 hands per hour. This means that you're putting through $3,000 per hour. You'll incur a $15-per-hour loss ($3,000 x -.5% = -$15) on the machine. But now add the 1% cash rebate (1% because of double points). That's $30 back. Simply having a slot club card in the machine's reader raises the expected return to 100.5% (99.5% + 1%), which is a $15-per-hour *profit* instead of a $15-per-hour loss. That's a stunning turnaround!

So, in comparing one casino to another, you have to add the payback from the video poker machines and the cashback from the slot club. Before you get too excited (and really do quit your day job), keep in mind that it's rare to find full-pay machines in a casino with good cashback opportunities. Some casino slot clubs pay no cashback at all, only comps. Others pay a small percentage, .10%-.25% in cash, and the rest in comps. But if you keep your eyes and ears open and combine the good machines with cashback from a good slot club, you'll often find yourself in positive land.

That's for video poker. Slot machines, of course, are rarely, if ever, a positive play. Still, many casino slot clubs return more in comps and cashback for slot play than for video poker play. No matter what kind of gambling machine you like to play, you'll always do better with a slot club card inserted.

A Textbook Case in Tunica

An experience we had at the Hollywood Casino in Tunica will give you an idea of how you can gather information to analyze the potential of a new slot club.

Things were made easier, since the Hollywood's slot club had a brochure at the booth that provided a lot of the information we needed. It told us that at sign-up, we'd be given a qualifying card called the Screen Test card. As soon as we earned 400 points, we could go back to the booth, where they'd give us a T-shirt and the Marquee Card, signifying that we'd become full members.

The brochure also revealed exactly what we needed to know about redeeming points, including how much they were worth. We saw that every 10 points at the Screen Test level were redeemable for one dollar. At the Marquee level, points were worth $1.50. The one thing it didn't tell us was how much money we had to put through the machine to earn each point. So we tested the card in different machines. We tried 25¢ video poker and found that we had to play 120 quarters (or

$30) to get one point. The 25¢ slots only required 100 quarters ($25) to get that same point. Then we checked the dollar slots ($20) and dollar video poker ($25).

We now had enough information to go off into a corner and figure out what percentage this worked out to. At the initial Screen Test level, 25¢ video poker paid back a .33% cash rebate, while $1 video poker paid back .4%. At the Marquee level, video poker paid .5% and .6%, respectively (a relatively small difference between quarters and dollars). We also noticed a sign advertising double points during the week we were there. So instead of 25¢ machines adding .5% to the payoff and dollars .6%, we could earn a full 1% for quarters and 1.2% for dollars.

Then we looked at the choice of video poker machines. The Hollywood had no machines that returned over 100%. The best quarter video poker was an 8/5 progressive, but the royal flush had just been hit causing the royal flush jackpot to reset at $1,000. At this level, the return was a dismal 97.3% that no slot club rebate could save. There were 9/6 Jacks or Better machines at the dollar level.

We had already checked out the video poker schedules and slot club benefits in all the other Tunica-area casinos and found nothing on the 25¢ level that would give us any better than a breakeven or slightly positive game. Although we preferred to play quarters, we decided we could not pass up this positive opportunity for dollars. The .8% slot club rebate at the Screen Test level put the 9/6 Jacks or Better at 100.3%. And when we achieved the Marquee level (which we'd do quickly, with both of us playing dollars on the same account), we'd earn a 1.2% slot club rebate and be playing at 100.7%. In addition, we knew we'd accrue enough points playing dollars to get our room free, along with full food comps wherever we wanted to eat. We would have been happy with our $42-per-hour theoretical expected return (600 hands x $5 per hand = $3,000 per hour through the machine x 100.7% expected return = $21 x two players = $42), but Lady Luck decided to give us a $4,000 royal flush this visit, which meant we "earned" quite a bit more.

As Good As It Gets

As I discussed earlier, the Stardust was one of our core slot clubs when we first became low rollers. Every month, like clockwork, the mail brought us some sort of great offer from them — free food, free rooms, free merchandise. We always looked forward to the invitations to their car giveaways, which they conducted several times a year. In late 1994, the Stardust sent us an offer for three free nights and 500 drawing tickets for the January contest. There were hundreds of thousands of tickets in the huge drum, all given to reward long-term slot club members for their loyal regular play. Nine of ten tickets pulled would receive cash prizes from $500 to $1,000. The tenth, the first ticket drawn, would win the car.

I'd been sick in bed all that day, but since you had to be present to win, I dragged myself down to the casino and leaned against a wall, trying to keep from being smothered by the hordes of people milling around waiting to hear those lucky numbers. I figured it would turn out to be a waste of my energy — there were thousands of tickets in the drum. But persistence does pay. I got the ultimate slot club benefit when one of my tickets was the first drawn and I won a 1995 Mercury Mystique, plus $3,000 cash to help pay the taxes. It doesn't get much better than that!

"48 Hours" Interlude

In early 1995 the television newsmagazine "48 Hours" was planning a show on gambling and chose Brad and me to represent the "little guy" gambler—the low roller. This was our "15 minutes of fame" (actually, it was only 10). Two cameramen and an assistant producer flew from the CBS offices in New York to our home in Indianapolis where they started taping our every move as we packed and went to the airport. They documented our efforts to get bumped from each connecting flight, then flew with us to Vegas. They stayed in the same hotel we did, though they paid $70 a night, while our room, of course, was free.

Because the casinos are deathly afraid of negative publicity, most would not grant the crew permission to film us in action, so we all went "undercover." The cameramen had tiny cameras in their caps and I was given a special pair of glasses with a camera in the nosepiece. They fitted me with what I called my "terrorist" vest, the inside pockets full of wires and recorders. Two more producers joined us, plus the on-camera correspondent, Susan Spencer.

We led them on a five-day casino assault mission into our world of positive-expectation video poker, comps, and couponing. They filmed us day and night, right up to the time we fell into bed, exhausted, each night! They said we "spoiled" Vegas for their after hours—they wanted to gamble but they'd learned just enough that they knew they would be making "bad" bets.

On the last day they followed us as we checked into the Stardust. I was so tired that I was giddy. With the hidden cameras rolling, I pranced around a Mercury Mystique in the lobby area and jested, "Film me with this car. I'm going to win it in the next drawing."

Two days later it was time for the drawing. I was

sick, but determined to attend. Brad said I was out of my head. We'd been in many of these big-ticket drawings and hadn't even won a small "last-place" prize. The "48 Hours" people weren't even there—blessedly, the whole crew had left town to go back to New York.

The "impossible" happened. My ticket was pulled out first and that shiny new Mercury Mystique was really mine. When we notified "48 Hours," they flew out two cameramen who taped our limo ride from the casino to the dealership to choose the color of car we wanted, and to take delivery.

It was an ending worthy of a made-for-TV story, titled "Lady Luck."

"48 Hours" Inside Edition

Editor's Note: The following, excerpted from the March 1995 Las Vegas Advisor, *provides an inside look at how Jean Scott wound up on national television and what happened during the taping. It's written by Anthony Curtis.*

I was contacted by "48 Hours" point people in November 1994. They'd heard about Max Rubin's [book] *Comp City*, and wanted to make comps one of their show's primary topics. A meeting was arranged at Luxor with Max, me, and the segment's producer in attendance. The idea coming in was that Max would discuss comps on camera, then play in the casino and bag a gourmet dinner or a show. The producer wasn't completely sold that this was a story for America. "How," he asked, "would the average tourist relate?"

"People will relate," I said. "Comps are for everyone; that's why Max wrote the book. There's a comp for every man and every budget."

"Every man? That's what we need here, an 'every-man' to demonstrate that this really can be done by someone who's not a pro."

"The Queen?" Max looked at me.

"Yeah, the Queen."

We described a few of Jean's exploits and the producer was sold. In an instant, comps became an aside, and the Queen was contacted to see if she would trade a little of her Las Vegas anonymity for a true 15 minutes of fame. She was willing and the timing was good (her annual holiday trip was scheduled for the week of the taping.)

A camera crew was dispatched to her home in the Midwest to tape her packing. They then accompanied her to the airport to record her (unsuccessful) attempt at getting bumped off the flight to Las Vegas. In Las Vegas, the cameras followed her through 48 hours (actually pieced together over several days) of her best moves: coupon plays, special invites, drawing entries, slot club benefit redemptions, and the maintenance of her slot club accounts via expert play on video poker machines with high-yield schedules.

Here, though, the Queen ran into trouble. As fate would have it, she came up against a particularly nasty dry spell (she was down more than $2,000) and the cameras were rolling.

The Queen was depressed. "Why now?" she lamented over the phone.

"There's nothing you can do about it," I told her. "Besides, it doesn't hurt for the public to see a down side."

Easy for me to say. I wasn't the one getting my bankroll kicked on national television, and I wasn't the producer of a program showing people how to contribute to the building fund of the next megaresort. I did, however, know the Queen's track record. And I could, in good conscience, support her methods and attest to her long-run success.

Of course, it ain't over till it's over, especially in Las Vegas. Just when it looked like she would book a sure loser — POW! — the Queen popped a drawing at the Stardust to win a 1995 Mercury Mystique (sticker price $16,000) and $3,000 cash. "48 Hours" got its story. The Queen got her glory (and a Mystique).

Was she lucky? Sure she was, at least in terms of the timing. But the car, or a car somewhere down the road, was part of the Queen's expected result. Her master plan includes entering contests and getting her name in drawings, then following up any way she can to enhance her chances. At the Stardust, for example, she'd done everything the rules would allow to get as many tickets in the drawing drum as possible. And she remained diligent, even in the midst of a losing streak compounded by a debilitating flu, by dragging herself downstairs at drawing time because entrants had to be present to win. By constantly putting herself in a position to win things and get things, she ultimately does.

What happened between the Queen and the car is another whole story. After long days of advanced maneuvering, she managed to resell the Mystique, earning (after taxes) $1,200 more than the $9,000 cash offered by the Stardust in lieu of the car. In her typical fashion, she managed to parlay a big win into an even bigger win.

6

Comps
Your Just Desserts

Is there anyone out there in gambling land who doesn't know what the word "comp" means? Comp is short for "complimentary," which means free — my all-time favorite word. In the casino (and travel) biz, complimentaries refers to free rooms, free food, free airfare, and other free amenities that make up a gambling or travel vacation.

Almost everyone has heard exciting high-roller stories, or at least seen a movie where a tuxedo-clad Sean Connery or Robert Redford bets with $100,000 chips and stays in magnificent penthouse suites and takes day trips on luxurious yachts and eats fabulous gourmet meals. Because of these images, I suspect that most people connect comps only with high rollers. They say to themselves, "I'm not a big bettor so I could never get any comps." That's about the farthest thing from the truth that I can think of in the gambling business. Comps are available to all players. Low rollers just have to scale down their sights a little.

Sure, you can have penthouse suites with in-room

Jacuzzis, towels so thick that you can hardly wrap them around yourself, and casino personnel fawning over you at every turn. All you have to do is make $5,000 bets all weekend long. On the other hand, comps for low rollers are probably even better from a proportional standpoint. After all, you can only sleep in one room at a time, and I doubt that most people sleep any better if their bathroom fixtures are gold-plated. Likewise, you can only eat so much a day, and most people wouldn't want to eat their three squares in a gourmet room even if they could. For that matter, if you stay in hotel-casinos a long time as we used to do, or are a Vegas local as we are now, I can guarantee that you wouldn't even want to eat in a gourmet room every night.

Comps can move you quickly to higher levels of the gambling pyramid. If you're already playing a positive-expectation game, then comps are the gravy. However, for most people, getting comps is a way to make up the losses from their negative-expectation play. The purpose of this chapter is to show you how you can get comps—more comps than you could imagine—even though you're a small bettor. I'll share some of our secrets for living the champagne life on a peanut-butter-and-jelly budget.

The Universal Comp

What's the most common comp that the casino gives? One that anyone can get? You guessed it—free drinks. Play any game—table or machine—in a casino and before long a cocktail waitress will come around and offer you a drink. In fact, you don't always have to be gambling. I don't suggest you abuse this loophole, but you'll probably be offered free drinks if you're sitting at a slot machine or in a keno lounge or in a race and sports book and only look like you're gambling.

You can stand at a crap table or sit behind a poker table watching a friend play and cocktail waitresses will usually include you in the free-drink order. You can get by on this ploy as long as you don't look like a homeless person trying to escape the elements and don't try to do it for long periods of time.

This drink comp can vary greatly in value, depending on your drinking habits. Since I can't have alcohol for health reasons, I usually drink diet soda, but how many diet sodas can any one person drink in a day? I run up the comp value by ordering expensive bottled water to bring back to our room, or an exotic tropical (virgin) concoction that would cost a bundle in any restaurant.

If you like alcoholic drinks, you can really increase the value of the comp (except in a few places where the law does not allow casinos to give away free alcoholic beverages, such as Illinois riverboats and some Indian casinos) by ordering call brands, such as Chivas Regal, Stolichnaya, Bailey's, and Captain Morgan.

Now is probably a good time to discuss tipping. Although the drinks are free and you're not required to tip, the custom is to do so. If you choose not to, be prepared for the cocktail waitress to visit you less often (and probably display a chilly attitude when she does). Deciding how much to tip has always been a quandary for me. I am, by nature, a very thrifty (some say miserly) person, and I have a natural tendency to undertip. Brad, on the other hand, is very generous and his rule is, "When in doubt, give more." Between us, we probably average out to the right level.

Here are some guidelines formulated from our experiences and from ideas I've gathered by talking to other players. It's accepted practice to base your tips on how much you're betting. Slot players might take one to four coins out of the tray per drink ordered—15¢ or

20¢ for nickel players, 25¢ to $1 for quarter players, $1 or $2 for dollar players. Most table players and many machine players have a flat-tip policy, no matter what they're betting, because they feel the cocktail waitress does the same amount of work for every drink. Other people tip less when they're losing and more when they're winning. And some always tip big because they like special attention from the waitresses or it puts them in a "sporty" mood (makes them feel like they're having more fun). Other people feel it's wasteful to pay more for a "free" drink than they would by buying it at a bar. I like this general rule: tip nothing for surly service, on the low end for mediocre service, and on the high end for cheerful service.

Comps for Machine Players

In the last chapter, I discussed the comps a machine player—slots or video poker—can get by joining slot clubs. These comps—for food, rooms, shows, and merchandise—are sometimes built right into the slot club payoff structure. From a list in the brochure, you can choose to "spend" the points that you earn on food, rooms, or shows, redeem for cashback, or take merchandise.

Some clubs have dual systems. Your point balance that comes up on the card reader can be used for cash and/or merchandise, but there is another "bank" in which you accumulate comp credits. For every point you earn toward cashback, you also earn a comp point that can be used for room nights, food, and shows.

Sometimes a casino awards the cashback according to a set schedule, then mails out comp offers that vary, depending on your recent play and the time of year.

In all of the above systems, the comps are openly offered to you—all you have to do is use them. How-

ever, the casinos that have such forthright programs
are definitely in the minority. Usually you have to pry
things out of the casinos. Your most powerful tool in
doing this is that tiny three-letter word: "ask." I can't
emphasize how important this word is. No matter how
little or how much the casino offers you, you can get
more if you ask. In fact, if you don't ask, you may not
get anything at all.

Eating Free

You've heard the expression, "There's no such
thing as a free lunch." Well, in a casino there is — and
a free breakfast and a free dinner, too.

When we started visiting Las Vegas, it was as if
we were in the kindergarten of comp school. That was
21 years ago. So you could say that we've graduated
high school and are now at the college level. We've
made great strides, but there's still a lot to learn. This
is especially true of the food-comp situation.

If the slot club has food comps built right into the
system and the schedule says that a buffet costs 50
points, all you have to do is step up to the slot club
booth to get it. However, as I've warned you, the printed literature doesn't always tell you what it takes to get
your meals comped (and neither do the slot club booth
personnel). In these cases, it takes a lot of experience to
know what you have to do to get free food. Allow me
to share some of my experiences with you.

When we first joined the Stardust slot club after
we switched from blackjack to video poker, and for a
year or so after, we knew about cash rebates, as well as
free-room and occasional free-meal offers sent through
the mail. But we figured that was it. One day I was getting a cash rebate at the slot club booth when I heard
someone at the next window say that they would like

a comp for two to the buffet. What was this? There was nothing in the literature, nothing on any sign, no indication whatsoever that food comps (obtained at the booth) were part of the bargain. I asked how many points it took to get a food comp, and I was told that you could get a buffet for two after earning 150-200 points. I was thrilled, of course, to find out about this new comp opportunity, and further elated to discover that the comp didn't reduce my point balance. But I remember being puzzled by the "ballpark" figure. Why didn't the slot club just specify that a buffet comp for two cost 150 points or 200 points? One or the other? Why the 50-point spread? Since then I've learned that the food-comp situation is nebulous.

The criteria for getting food comps vary enormously, and I don't just mean from casino to casino. They vary from employee to employee, and even from one day to the next depending on the mood of the same person! Sometimes it's better to ask the clerk at the slot club. Other times it's better to ask a slot host. But in all cases, it goes back to that key strategy I've emphasized again and again: ask someone.

If you're not familiar with the slot club's policy on food comps and they're not built into the schedule, start at the slot club booth and ask how you might get a buffet comp. You ask for a buffet because that's the lowest food comp level. It costs the casino the least amount of money to feed you there, so it gives the new player the best shot at a free meal. If you're told, "Well, you have 100 points in your account, but you need to have 200 points for a meal comp," that's OK. Now you know that you'll have to play about four hours of 25¢ video poker instead of just two to get your free meal at that casino.

What if you go to the slot club booth, ask for a meal comp, and the clerk there says "No," or "I don't know," or just acts too busy to bother with you? Well, I never stop there. I go back to my machine and start playing again. Then, as soon as a change person comes around, I ask if she can send over a slot club host. Pretty soon, one will appear. I'll say I've been playing so many hours and we'd like to eat. Then I ask, "What does it take to get a buffet?" I always ask for anything I want in that way. "What does it take" to get something? If you say, "Can I have a buffet?" and you can't, the situation gets uncomfortable. The slot host doesn't like to say "No," and you certainly don't want to hear "No." Most people get embarrassed by the whole exchange and wish that they'd never asked in the first place. Worse, they're less likely to ask in the future. But if you phrase it in such a way that neither yes nor no is called for, you've put the host in a position where he can give you any number of answers, all of which will give you some valuable information.

The host will probably say that he needs to check his records. He'll ask for your slot club membership number, then disappear to check you out in some dark and mysterious computer place. He may come back with a buffet comp all written up and hand it to you. Then you'll know that you never have to play longer than three hours (or however long). In fact, you could even ask at that time exactly how long you needed to play.

The host might come back and say that you have 100 points now, and as soon as you have 150 points you should ask again. Now you know what it takes. Rarely, when you phrase your request as I've recommended, will a host return and say that you can't get a buffet without giving you an idea of how far you have to go to earn it. There's always a point at which you've played long enough to get free food in any casino. You just have to find out what that point is.

While you're talking with a booth clerk or a host, you can also try to find out what it takes to eat in the coffee shop or gourmet restaurant. Feel your way around it. Find out where the break points are for the different levels of food comps. We've learned that, when it comes to comps, it pays to ask more than one person in the casino. I can't count the number of times I've gotten different answers to the same question from different casino personnel. The slot club booths are often staffed by overworked employees who, at best, are nice but harried, and at worst, don't know and don't care. Even slot hosts (both men and women are called "hosts"), who are supposedly hired for their ability to deal with the public, vary greatly in their knowledge and social skills. Also, casinos vary tremendously in how much latitude they allow their personnel in granting comps. We treasure finding the right hosts in the right casinos.

This brings us to the subject of attitude—yours. Don't be demanding or unpleasant. Be nice! An old adage applies double in the casinos: Honey draws more flies than vinegar. Do things that will make the job of the person who can do things for you easier. If you do it right, you'll be subtly telling them that you know they don't just give out this food for nothing. You know that they want (and expect) you to play at their casino. You're just asking what they expect you to do to be able to get whatever it is you want. It'll pay dividends.

Back when we played quarters and stayed in hotel-casinos for long periods of time, people always wanted to know how many hours a day we played to be able to get all of our meals free. Because comps tend to be based on long-term play history as well as current play, it gets easier to qualify for comps as time goes by. On average, we used to play about eight hours a day between the two of us and found that this qualified us for more meals than we could possibly consume. However, a new player might want to start out with a goal of getting just one meal a day—a buffet—and slowly learn the requirements to get more meals in the buffet and coffee shop and better meals in the more exclusive eateries.

Now, you might say that you can't be bothered going to all this trouble, especially since the buffet is often only $10 or so. You might reason that it's so cheap to begin with, even cheaper than eating at home, that there's no point in having to ask for a free one. Well, I'll tell you the reasons why I go to the trouble.

First, I try never to pay for anything that I can get for free, no matter how small the amount is. It's part of the fun I have doing what I do in the casinos.

Second, I don't like to wait in lines. I can't tell you how many long buffet lines I've seen in Las Vegas where people wait for more than an hour to get in. In most cases there's a comp line that's a lot shorter than the regular line. Occasionally, especially at off-Strip casinos that cater to locals, the comp line is longer than the regular line (because they give out so many buffet comps). In that event, take your comp and stand in the regular line. There's no rule saying that comps can't go through the regular line, only that someone without a comp can't go through the comp line.

There's a third good reason for getting a comp. Everyone likes to feel important. I don't care if it's the lowliest buffet in Las Vegas, when I step into that comp line, I feel a little more important than I do when I'm in the regular line, especially when the sign says "VIP Line" or "Invited Guests." It's just a little classier and it feels good.

And here's a fourth reason. When you stay for long periods of time, these smaller comps add up. Less of your cash spent on food means money you can keep in your gambling bankroll.

Sleeping Free

Bagging free rooms takes a bit more play on the machines than getting free food. Like food comps, room comps are built into many slot club reward systems or offered in mailings on a fairly regular basis. But more often, these free nights only materialize when you dig for them.

It's possible that the employees at the slot club booth might be helpful with some information, but usually, rooms must be taken care of either by a slot host or someone in the slot marketing office. Established customers with previous slot club play can often call ahead and ask for "slot club reservations." Sometimes this is the regular reservation desk and the agent has access to the computer records of your play and is authorized to give you free nights according to a set schedule. More often, the slot club has its own department to handle member reservations (perhaps with a separate 800 number). In either case, this is a good place to ask about the requirements for free rooms. I've found that I get the most detailed information on room comps from these phone employees.

Of course, getting rooms absolutely free is the ultimate. But getting discounted rooms (especially when the city is busy) ain't bad either. This is where even the beginning comp seeker can strike gold. There are several different levels of discounted rooms. In my experience almost all hotels will give you the discounted "casino rate" (usually 40%-50% off the rack rate) if you're a member of the slot club, some even if you have never played on their card. Some require just a small point minimum. This is another reason to join as many slot clubs as you can.

The only time you should ever have to pay the scandalously high rack rate for a room in a hotel-casino might be on your very first visit. And you can try to avoid it even then if you call and ask the slot club if you can join by phone or by mail in advance. Sometimes you can sign up on the casino's Web site. Even if you find that you must book your reservation at a non-discounted rate, all is not lost. As soon as you check in, get a slot club card, put some play on it, then see a slot host. Find out the requirements for the casino rate and perhaps a free night or two. Hosts have the authority to change your room rate just before you check out. Go ahead and ask—it's money in your pocket (or credit on your credit card).

Another slot club weapon a beginner (or even an old pro) can use is the one against a "sold-out" sign. You can often get a room at a hotel on a busy weekend when the regular reservations clerk tells you that the joint is completely booked. Almost all casinos hold back blocks of rooms for their slot club members. Either call the slot club direct or tell the reservations clerk that you belong to the slot club. You'll be pleasantly surprised when a room materializes where there was no room before.

Free Shows

To get tickets for casino shows, use the same techniques discussed earlier. If show comps aren't built into the point system, again you'll just have to inquire. You'll usually be more successful asking a slot host rather than a booth clerk. Most important, though, is the timing of your request. It's easier to get free tickets for a weekday show or during months when business is slow; the casinos don't like their showrooms empty and entertainers perform better to a full room. Don't try for tickets to a popular show on a Friday or Saturday night, or over a holiday weekend, when paying customers fill the seats, unless you're a fairly heavy player.

A "sold-out" show, however, doesn't necessarily represent an insurmountable barrier. Just as they do with rooms, casinos set aside blocks of seats for comps. Of course, high rollers get first consideration, but Brad and I have been able to get seats to a sold-out show by asking the slot host as late as 15 minutes before showtime.

Unusual Comps

You can get comped for almost anything in Vegas. Most people think of comps as free food, free rooms, and free shows, but that's just the beginning of the story. We've been comped Christmas presents for our grandchildren. We've been comped a $250 life-sized stuffed gorilla that sits proudly in the back of our car. I've been a redhead, a blonde, and a brunette thanks to beauty-shop comps, and I've had manicures, pedicures, facials, and massages. We've gotten jewelry and clocks. We've gotten free roller coaster rides and movies.

The Par-A-Dice riverboat in Illinois once offered phone cards on its list of things that you could get with points (300 points to get a two-hour phone card). Those 300 points could be redeemed for $3 in cashback. So instead of getting $3 cash, I got phone cards instead. Why? Phone calls cost about 10¢ a minute back then, so my 300 points were worth $12 this way. In fact, I got double because I used mine to make daytime business calls that cost 20¢ a minute. Now I was getting eight times the cash-back rate for my slot points!

No-Slot-Club Comps

A few casinos still don't have slot clubs. These are smaller casinos where the owners don't want to make the big investment in equipment and personnel necessary to start and maintain a slot club, or where the managers just don't believe in their value. How do you get comps when you're playing in a casino that doesn't have a slot club?

It's very simple. Do you recall how I told you to ask for comps when they're not built into the slot club system? Well, that's the same way you do it when the casino doesn't have a slot club at all. It usually takes no more than three hours of quarter video poker play, four hours at the most, to get a buffet at these places, too. If two of you are playing, you could probably play for two hours apiece and get the buffet comped.

In these places, you'll also want to ask if there's anything other than simply playing that you have to do. For example, sometimes you have to get a change person to tell a supervisor that you've played so many hours. Sometimes you have to keep a coin buy-in tracking card. But in most casinos that don't have a slot club or any other way to track your play, they'll usually just take your word for it. I've gone in and played video poker for two hours in a casino that didn't have a slot club and then sought out a supervisor and said, "We've been playing here two hours and we're hungry now and want to eat. Have we qualified for a comp yet?" She simply took my word for it, appearing not to be too worried about getting cheated out of two buffets.

Comps for Table Game Players

A lot of the information in the first half of this chapter about how machine players get comps is also useful for table players. In fact, more and more casinos are going to a whole-casino comp system, because they realize that many people play both the machines and the tables, and many couples want to combine one person's machine play with the other's table time in order to maximize their comps.

However, most casinos haven't integrated their slot and table-game comp systems fully, though many now encourage their table players to show a slot club card for faster rating purposes. In most places, you give the card to the pit boss, who sets up a separate table-game account for you. Sometimes the pits use the same slot club account number and enter their information into the same computer records that log your machine play. This allows someone from either the slot department or the pit to take into account all play and award comps accordingly.

The majority of casinos, however, still deal with table players the old-fashioned way. Even though the information eventually gets into a computer (in some form), the initial fact-gathering is done by a very human pit boss who has to rate you. So, when you sit down at a blackjack, crap, roulette, or baccarat table, the key to getting comps is getting noticed.

One way to get noticed is to bet really large amounts of money. "Really large" is relative. In Vegas it could mean thousands of dollars a hand in an upscale casino like the Mirage, or green-chip ($25) play downtown at the El Cortez. Two green chips at most of the mid-range casinos in any gambling area will get you noticed. That's the easiest way to get comps. At a lot of places, the pit boss will keep mental track of your play and write you a coffee shop comp if you ask when you're ready to leave.

But what about true low rollers? What if you're a $5 bettor, $10-$15 at the most? Can you get a comp? The answer is a resounding "Yes," *if* you pick casinos in what we call the mid-level range. It's fairly easy to figure—just cross out the most luxurious resorts in any casino area. Every casino has a set policy about the minimum bet it'll track from the pit. Again, that good little word "ask" will help you out here. At any table game in any casino, tell the dealer you want to speak with the pit boss. When he comes up, you simply ask, "What is the minimum tracking bet here?" The boss will probably look at your bet and let you know if it's big enough. If it is, he'll probably ask if you want to be rated. He'll take your name, or sometimes he'll ask you to fill out a card with your name, address, and other information. If you already have a slot club card from the casino, give that to him.

Again, if you're not a card counter or a cheat playing under an alias, you shouldn't care that the casino has your name and address; in fact, you want the casinos to have them. Every time a casino takes this information, you're increasing your chances of getting something, whether it's a comp on the spot or some kind of offer that comes later in the mail. Take it from someone who's given her name and address to dozens of casinos around the world over a 21-year period. I've never gotten anything but good news from them. They almost always want to give me something!

The pit boss will take your information and, more often than not, type it into the pit computer, which holds the casino's player database (or he'll give it to the pit secretary to input into the computer). Your name and address will be entered, as well as what seat position you're occupying (i.e., seat one at blackjack table two) and how much you're betting. The higher you bet, the more you'll get. Also, the more you bet, the less time you'll have to play to get what you want in comps. So it's important to be rated for as high a bet as possible, and as I'm sure you were expecting me to tell you, there are ways to get rated for betting larger amounts than you actually do.

Let's say you plan to be betting between $5 and $15. As soon as you get noticed by the pit boss, put out your biggest bet—three red chips. Don't stack them neatly; let the pit boss see that there are three chips there, not just two; this is the most important information you can give the pit boss for *your* purposes. Now, don't go overboard by putting down $50, then playing $5 the rest of the time. That's too obvious, and will probably make the dealer and the pit boss suspicious. Remember, you're a low roller. Stick with red chips, but put down three of them at first and then bet $5, $10, or $15 the rest of the time.

If the joint is hopping, or even if it's not busy and the pit boss isn't worried about you because it's a place where most of the players are nickel bettors, he may never look at you again. You can bet $5, one red chip, for the rest of the night, however many hours you play, and still be marked down as a $15 bettor.

Sometimes the boss goes around holding a little slip of paper with all the names of everyone being rated. You'll know when he's doing this: he's got the slip of paper (or his clipboard or notebook) and he's looking at the chips in action on all of the tables in his section. If you see him at the next table writing down bets—and you should see him because you want to keep an eye on the boss (discreetly, of course) so you know when he's looking at you—you'll need to crank up your bets to $15 again. You want it set in his mind that you're a $15 bettor, even though your average is lower.

Closing the Deal

After you've played no more than an hour, call the pit boss over again and say, "I'm getting kind of hungry. How much longer do I need to play to get a buffet for my friend and me?" (If you can't catch the pit boss' attention naturally as he walks by, or you feel shy, tell your dealer that you want to speak with him.) He'll probably have to check you out in the computer, since he likely wasn't paying that much attention to you. When he checks, he'll see that you've been playing an hour and that he has you down as a $15 bettor.

If you're in a small or mid-sized place, there's a good chance he'll come back and say, "You can have a comp right now." Take it. Tell him that you'll play a little longer and then go eat. On the other hand, the boss might come back and say that you need to play another hour for a comp. That's fine. After another 45 minutes, ask again. That's close enough to an hour and he will probably give it to you.

Can you see why it's important to give your name and get rated? If you sit down and play blackjack or any other table game for four hours and don't give your name to the pit boss, he might not notice you at all. Now when it comes time to ask for something, you'll be at a big disadvantage. Plus, the same pit boss isn't always on duty during your play. The bosses go to dinner or on break; the shifts change. If you call the relief boss over and ask for a comp, he'll definitely check the records. But if you didn't ask to be rated, there won't be any record to check. The best thing that can happen now is that the pit boss will ask you how long you've been playing and maybe take your word for it. Don't stretch the truth when you're asked, because he may ask the dealer for verification. If you claim you've been there several hours when you've really been there 45 minutes, the dealer will usually let the pit boss know.

Most of the time in these cases the boss'll say that he doesn't know how long you've been playing and tell you that he'll start rating you now; after you've played for another few hours he'll give you a comp. Because you didn't give the joint your name four hours ago, you have to start back at zero on the comp clock.

An important rule of thumb for food comps is to ask for them the same day you earn them, or at least during the same visit. Slot club records are usually kept indefinitely if you play just a couple of times during the year. But records from the tables are deleted from the computer after a short time, especially for small bettors. It's all but impossible to get a food comp for your play six months ago, even if you received no comps then. The pit likes current action.

The comp system for table players is based on the ability of the pit to track your play, so it's in your best interests to make it easy for them to do that. They're usually unwilling to try to keep tabs on a player with a style of jumping from table to table every few minutes. It's okay to change tables after reasonable lengths of time (a half hour or more), but be sure to inform the pit boss when you do. If you're moving to another table in the same pit area, he can merely note your change of position. If you move to another pit, be sure to check in again with the new boss, so he can begin a new record. In some casinos, the tracking records don't get into the computer until the end of a shift or the next day, so you may have to inform the pit boss of your play earlier that day in other pits when requesting your comp.

Room Comps

While slot clubs have ensured that machine players now get what they have coming to them in the way of room discounts, I can't tell you how many table-game players I've talked to, even green-chip players, who always pay full retail for lodging. Why? Again, because they never ask to be rated. Back when we were playing red-chip blackjack, we often stayed free using the same techniques that we now use playing video poker. We got our names on the mailing lists and received plenty of offers for free rooms.

When you get rated, your name goes into the casino computer. When you're ready to go home, you can call casino marketing and say that you've been there for four days and played 16 hours (or whatever) of blackjack, and you're wondering if you can get a break on your room bill. If you've been rated, there's a chance that casino marketing will extend you the casino rate. If you've played a lot, you might even get your room free. This is true even if you're a $5 bettor. To the casino, making $5 bets for 10 hours is exactly the same as making $25 bets for two hours. Also, you can ask the casino to combine the action of your partner, if you're playing with a spouse or someone who shares your room, which makes it easier to end up with a higher rating.

Again, I'm going to keep pounding on this drum: ask, ask, ask. Remember the "Myths" chapter? In all my years of playing in casinos, I have never had a pit boss come up to me and tell me he'd like to comp my room. Not once. But I've had lots of rooms comped, because I've called casino marketing and asked if I could get a break on my bill.

Show Comps

Playing table games for relatively short periods of time is a good technique for getting show tickets, especially when you're not staying at the casino. Use the same timing hints that I gave you in the section for machine players. The amount you must bet and the length of time you'll be required to play will vary greatly depending on the show. To get tickets for *Celine Dion* at Caesars would take a bigger bankroll than most low rollers carry, but a $10 bettor at the Riviera could probably get two tickets to one of its shows in a couple of hours.

Tricks of the Comp Trade

After you've mastered the basics, there are all kinds of little things you can do to enhance your comp take on a small bankroll. For example, whenever possible, a man should ask a woman pit boss for a comp and a woman should ask a man. You'll almost always have better luck with a cross-gender move; this is also true for male and female slot hosts. It's just a little psychological manipulation. I'm almost embarrassed by the number of comps and favors I've gotten from male pit bosses, just because I've been friendly in a feminine sort of way. Brad just shakes his head in amazement when I ask for and get outrageously fine comps from the guys for such small play.

Here's another ploy. Since most table-game players are bucking negative expectation, the more they can limit their exposure to the house advantage, the better. That means playing as few hands as possible. After you've been clocked in, you don't have to stay seated at that table the whole time. One trick is to drink a lot (but I suggest your beverage of choice be nonalcoholic, so your judgment isn't clouded). That gives you an excuse for a lot of bathroom breaks. When you go, don't rush back to the table. The rating clock is always running. Wander around and people watch or go outside for a breath of fresh air. You can leave two or three times an hour and stay gone for five minutes or so at a time.

You can say things to the dealer such as, "Watch

my chips, I have to get rid of some of this coffee (juice/cola/beer …)." Or "I'm going to get a little air." Or "You know, I'm allergic to smoke and this smoke is really getting to me." (Don't use this if you're the one smoking!) You can also sit at a nonsmoking table and say, "Well, time for a smoke," even if you don't smoke. These are all logical reasons for leaving the table for periods of time. By taking two ten-minute breaks an hour, you wind up playing 40 hands instead of 60, but you get credit for playing all 60. Your bankroll will last longer, plus your mind and body will thank you for the breather.

These are only a few tricks of the comp trade. There's a whole book on the subject, an excellent one written by Max Rubin called *Comp City – A Guide to Free Las Vegas Vacations*. Although it emphasizes the high roller, dozens of the hints Max gives can be used effectively by low rollers, too. He tells you the best games to play for comps, how the casino calculates them, and how to get the most comps for the least betting action. Work Max's system diligently and you'll reap thousands of dollars in casino comps.

Are You Getting Your Share?

Here are some interesting statistics from a couple years back. Fully 72.8% of all the drinks dispensed in downtown Las Vegas were complimentary. Of all the meals served downtown, 38% were free. Things are a bit tighter on the Strip. Of all the drinks served in Strip casinos, 46.6% were free, and 18% of the meals were complimentary. As far as rooms are concerned, 29.6% of downtown's occupied rooms were comped, compared with 14.5% on the Strip.

A very small percentage of these comps were given to high rollers, because the number of high rollers in

Las Vegas compared to everyone else is very small. Most of the comps go to low rollers.

You say you're too shy or embarrassed to ask for comps? Remember that one of the pit bosses' and slot hosts' biggest responsibilities is to reward people who play in their casino so they'll feel good and come back (and the bosses and hosts will continue to have jobs). The casinos build their business on customer loyalty. They *want* to give you comps. You don't have to be loud or even pushy to get them. That powerful little word "ask," when used in a gentle and kindly way, can produce outstanding results.

A Caveat

Never bet more than you ordinarily would just to get a comp. The food in the most elegant $50 Sunday brunch will taste awfully bitter if you've lost $500 playing blackjack just to get it.

Play the games you always play. Bet the same amounts you ordinarily bet. Gamble no longer than you normally do. But get all the comps you have coming to you for your normal habits. Take advantage of the systems that have been put in place to give you your just rewards.

7

Promotions
Casino Gravy

When I began traveling to casino destinations, I took with me the same thrifty habits I'd developed over four decades of a patently frugal life. I'd always clipped grocery coupons to use at the supermarket. I scoured the newspapers daily to find sales and promotions. I bought entertainment-club books full of two-for-one dining and show discounts. "Free" has been my favorite word since childhood when I treasured the prize at the bottom of the Cracker Jack box. So it was second nature for me to search for bargains in Las Vegas, Atlantic City, and the other gambling venues.

It didn't take long to discover that gambling towns, especially Las Vegas, are a coupon-lover's paradise! Casinos give out more coupons than Procter and Gamble, Kellogg, and Gillette combined. Promotions are everywhere, all the time. For me, Las Vegas was Shangri-La, Xanadu, and the Big Rock-Candy Mountain all rolled into one. It was the promised Land of Ku Pon. And before long, I'd been crowned its Queen.

In those dizzying early years, I sped around like a

whirling dervish, taking advantage of every promotion I could find. I used every coupon that was worth anything at all, entered every drawing, and collected as much free merchandise as the casinos would give me. I'd make a special trip to an outlying casino on a shuttle bus for a free spin on a roulette wheel. I made it a point to play in casinos that awarded extras—logo caps, T-shirts, sweatshirts, jackets, drawing entries, even six packs of pop—when you hit four deuces or 4-of-a-kind or a royal.

I dragged Brad all over town to attend all the drawings I'd entered that required you to be present to win. Many was the time I forced myself to go down to a casino after a long day of running around so I'd be present at a drawing.

I scoured casinos looking for discarded funbooks, to the extent (much to Brad's dismay) of looking in wastebaskets; I only drew the line at digging through half-eaten mustard-laden trash. I'm not ashamed to admit it, because I still do it today if the pickin's are ripe (the coupons, not the garbage). It's not a casual thing to me to retrieve a funbook that contains $5-$10 worth of gambling coupons and some free merchandise thrown in. It's not pennies that I'm eyeing garbage cans for; it's bona fide dollar activity.

From the very beginning, promotions have been as important to our style of play as expert video poker strategy, slot clubs, and comps. They can give you a big boost in your climb to the higher levels of the gambling pyramid. Many times a good promotion can turn a negative-expectation game into a positive one. At the very least, capitalizing on promotions can cut your losses significantly.

The importance of promotions doesn't stop at their cash-making potential, either. Brad has a thing for casino jackets. He has at least 50 logo jackets, six for every outfit he could possibly put together. He'll even, on occasion, participate in a negative-expectation promotion (horrors!) if a chance to win a jacket is involved.

Promotions also account for a lot of the fun we have on the casino circuit. I'm going to play video poker anyway, so if the casino wants to give Brad a logo jacket to celebrate my hitting a royal flush, that's just an easy extra. If I get entries into a drawing for a car by hitting 4-of-a-kinds, that's free action just for doing what I do. That's why I like promotions: they offer a financial *and* a psychological lift.

These days I'm not as fanatical as I used to be, so I'm a little more selective about the promotions in which I participate. But I still get the old zip when I find one that warrants the investment of my time and money.

Stalking the Wild Promotion

Where do you learn about promotions? You learn about promotions in so many different places that the best advice I can give is always to look everywhere. Read everything. Scan the local newspapers every day, then go back and whip through them again, looking for casino advertisements. Read the ads closely to see what's going on. You might find that a casino is giving double points to slot club members during the Monday Night Football game, hoping to entice the women to play the slot machines while the men are watching football. (Stereotyping and sexism are alive and well in casinos.) Oftentimes, the only place to find really current information is in the newspapers, because the locals who read them are a large market for the casinos.

The second best place to look for promotions and coupons is in the free tourist magazines, also known as "freebie mags." Most gambling towns have one or two, but Las Vegas supports about a dozen of them. You can generally find them in racks at the airports around the rental car counters; I grab any I see so I can get right into my research only five minutes after arriving, and so I have something to read while we wait for the free shuttle to take us to our hotel. You can also find the freebie magazines around the casinos, often near the bell desk. If you don't see them, ask; sometimes there's a rack somewhere else. (Also look for racks of coupons. You'll see these racks at the rental car offices and counters, tourist information centers, and in motel lobbies.) Some of the freebie-mag companies have deals with the hotels to put their periodical in the hotel rooms.

Every time I pass a casino, I read the marquee. Casinos like to advertise special promotions on the signage in front: this week they're paying 2-1 (instead of 3-2) for blackjacks, or they're only charging a 3% commission (instead of the usual 5%) on the bank bet at baccarat, or they're giving away $50,000 in a cash drawing.

Every single casino I go into, I look around for banners advertising something special. I always snoop around the slot club booth, too, where there are often brochures, leaflets, and the like that inform you about current promotions.

Another way to learn about promotions is to cultivate local contacts. Locals know a lot about promotions all over town. I always try to talk to the people playing video poker around us. Most of the time the people are visitors who don't know diddly, but occasionally someone will tell me that she's playing here at Casino X today, but tomorrow she'll be over at Casino Y, which is giving out free sweatshirts for 4-of-a-kinds.

One of the best places to learn about promotions is in the *Las Vegas Advisor*. Their research department follows all the casino events closely, their writers know how to analyze returns and strategy, and the monthly format is good for alerting you to what's going on or coming up. Another good place to find them is in a weekly tabloid called *Gaming Today*, given away free on Tuesdays in most race and sports books.

As always, if you have online access, you can tap into more information about what's going on in real time in Las Vegas than you can read, let alone digest and participate in. Almost all casinos now have Web sites, on which they advertise current promotions. Consumer sites, such as www.LasVegasAdvisor.com, keep up-to-date lists of funbooks, coupons, bonus-point promotions, and the like, and are an excellent start to your search. Video poker sites, the local Las Vegas daily newspapers, weekly tabloids, and freebie magazines all have Web sites. Simply type Las Vegas promotions into any search engine — then be prepared to spend the rest of your evening wading through them all.

Though some promotions keep going and going and going (usually the less valuable ones), no promotion lasts forever and many are very short term. If it's extremely positive, a promotion might wind up being cancelled almost before it gets going, because the locals in the know hit it hard and burn it out.

I've seen casino promos that awarded cash bonuses on royal flushes, but the bonuses were so valuable that teams of video poker professionals set up a monopoly on them. A two-person team can tie up a good machine for as long as a promotion lasts by playing 12-hour shifts. Once in a while a great promo comes along that's worth upwards of $50 to $100 an hour to the players. Needless to say, these deals don't last too long, as the casino figures out fast that they're getting the short end of the stick. But if you're lucky enough to jump on one when it starts, you can reap the benefits. (The books and software in the Resource list are invaluable for analyzing these opportunities.)

What's In It for the Casinos?

Why do casinos sponsor promotions? For one reason only: to get people through the doors and get a shot at their bankrolls. You can have the best casino in the world and the most high-tech machines, but if no one is playing them, you're not making any money. There are lots of casinos in many gambling venues around the country and they all want your patronage. The casinos know that they'll lose money on some promotions, but they treat it as a marketing expense. They figure that the promotion will attract more people who'll spend enough money on the side — while they're waiting for the promotion or eating before or after the promotion — to more than cover the losses.

You might ask if it's right to go to a casino only to play its promotion and not hang around for the losing activities. Well, there is no rule that says you can't. The casinos know that some people will only come in for the promotion, then take the money and run. They also know that hundreds of other people will come for the promotion and stick around long enough to lose more than the promotion won them. I don't think you have to worry about abusing the system, as long as you follow the rules and don't try to take so much advantage that your activities become unethical (see the "Ethics" chapter).

General Considerations

Read the Rules

Take care to investigate all the details of the promotion. This is sometimes easier said than done. Hotel-casinos are run by large monolithic corporations in which the channels of communication can be less than efficient. Many promotions are developed in the marketing or casino management departments, but details don't filter down to the floor before the printing department has distributed the rules, via flyers in the casino or advertisements in the newspaper. So the players find themselves in a situation where they know more about the promotion than the people who are running it! Always ask as many casino people as you can collar to clarify anything that's unclear.

A few promotions are for locals only and you must show an in-state drivers license (or a utility bill). Far more often it's the other way around, and you'll need to show an out-of-state ID. At some, you'll have to show an out-of-state ID and a hotel room key. What if you're not staying in a hotel? I suggest you keep a key handy for such cases. These days most hotels have plastic cards for room keys. There's no name on it and you don't have to return it when you check out. It's a good idea to hang onto the plastic key card in case a good promo comes along and you're staying with a local friend or living in your RV (or sleeping in a ditch). Then you'll have one to show at a promotion.

Attitude

A valuable tip I can give you about promotions is to be really friendly to the staff that's handling the details, with an eye toward getting more than you might ordinarily. Perhaps a pit boss has to lay a token on you or a change person has to stamp a card or a host has to give you drawing entries. If you're nice, and if you tip generously, you stand a much better chance of getting some extra consideration. In a casino, more than anything else tips make the wheels spin and the cogs turn and the free stuff flow, and a little judicious greasing of the skids works more wonders than you can imagine. (See "Ethics and Gambling," pg. 187, for a discussion on "tipping vs. bribery.")

After 21 years of casino gambling experience, we have a whole casino wardrobe—sweatsuits, sweaters, caps, visors, and the omnipresent T-shirts; we've probably gotten several hundred of them over the years. We have a closet full of Las Vegas jackets that have been given to us. We have 16 jackets from just one casino (it shall remain unnamed to protect the guilty), which handed them out to blackjack players. Every time you got a natural blackjack, the pit boss stamped a promotional card. When the card was filled up with stamps, you got the jacket. We got real friendly with one of the pit bosses and he got pretty tired of punching one of our cards every dozen hands or so. Finally, he'd just punch it 20 or 30 times and tell us he knew we were *going* to get those blackjacks!

Timing

When you enter a promotion is often as critical as *if* or *how* you enter it. This is true of drawings, tournaments, and machine promos. If a free drawing goes on day in and day out at different times and has daily winners, one factor to consider is when there'll be the fewest entrants. For example, Lady Luck in Las Vegas once had a little drawing you could enter (with a coupon from the funbook) that took place every hour. On the even hours, one person's name was pulled out of the drawing drum and that person went into a "Whirlwind of Cash." This was a booth where money blew around and you tried to grab as much as you could. Because you had to be present to win, a lot of people didn't want to bother with it, so it paid to look in the drawing drum to see how many entries it was holding. The fewer the entries, the better your chance of being picked.

In most drawings, the bigger the prize, the more entries you'll have to contend with. When the prizes are small, there are fewer entries. Another consideration for drawings is how often they empty the drum that holds the entries. Some casinos empty it after every drawing; others leave the entries in until the drum is near to bursting. And, of course, you have to pay attention to whether or not you have to be present to win. We enter many of them. It's fun to be chosen and with fewer entrants, there's a better chance of having your name drawn. We've been picked many times and it's always a thrill.

The Four Queens once sponsored a blackjack tournament called "King of the Hill." The qualifying rounds ran till late in the evening. If we waited till near the end, by checking the posted scores we could tell what score we had to beat. If the high score was too high, we wouldn't enter that day. If the high score was comparatively low, we would enter, and often adjust our playing strategy accordingly.

The better video poker promotions often attract the pros and promotion-happy folks who like to show up an hour or two before the start of the event. These people lock up the machines they want to use to play the promotion. If you show up near the starting time, there might not be any machines available, or you might have to play on one of the lesser-paying machines. The early bird gets the worm here.

When Not to Play a Promotion

There are basically two kinds of promotions: those that don't carry risk and those that do. A lot of promotions are free, and hence, riskless. But to participate in other promotions, you have to put up some money and gamble. So, a word of warning. Be sure the promotion that you want to play is good enough to cover the risk you're taking on; remember that whenever you participate in a promo where there's gambling involved, there are no guarantees. You may lose money.

Here's an example. It's pretty extreme, but you'll get the idea. The Barbary Coast in Las Vegas once had a blackjack deal that was one of the best promotions we've ever participated in. If you put up $5,000 cash, you got $5,400 worth of special non-negotiable chips to play at the tables. You had to play these chips (in order to have them switched out for regular chips that could be cashed in), so there was a great deal of risk. The Barbary Coast has a good blackjack game, so getting the free $400 was worth the risk to us. This promotion wasn't for the faint of heart. In fact, we know someone who ended up losing several thousand dollars. It happens. Don't risk it happening to you if you can't afford to lose the money.

A wise gambling consumer never participates in a promotion where it's necessary to risk more money than he would just by going about his normal gambling business. A coupon, a discount, a bonus—for any one of these to be valuable to you, you must be able to participate in the promotion and have a shot at getting something on top of what you would come away with just by gambling in an ordinary way.

Also, just because a casino is running a promotion doesn't mean that it's positive. If it's free, then it is (though it may be worth only fractions of a penny in expected return). But if there's a fee, you'll have to analyze the payback to determine if you're in positive land, or if the casino is trying to suck you into doing something that you wouldn't ordinarily do.

Another good reason not to participate in a promotion is if you hate the game. A friend of mine hates bingo more than anything. She'd rather have her teeth drilled without novocaine than sit in a smoky room with ten bingo cards and a messy dauber in front of her listening to someone drone, "B-fourteen; fourteen under B. O-sixty-eight; sixty-eight under O." She's a good candidate to pass up a bingo promotion, even if it is free.

One last reason not to play is if a promotion is too time-consuming, boring, or aggravating. For example, in Las Vegas there are a few locations on the Strip, as well as in casinos, where hawkers try to get you to attend a sales presentation for timeshare apartments or vacation clubs. They'll offer to reward you for your time with free show tickets. I liked their premiums, but after we'd attended about 20 of these presentations and gotten free shows and rooms and gifts, Brad finally put his foot down and told me that he didn't care what the freebie was, he was never going to listen to a 90-minute timeshare sales pitch again. And we never have.

Piggy-Backing

It's great when you can take advantage of more than one promotion at a time. One Las Vegas casino had a promotion involving a type of bingo card. Every time you hit a jackpot over a certain amount, you got a stamp from a change person. After collecting so many stamps, you got a cash rebate. At the same time that we were playing video poker and getting our bingo card stamped, we were also participating in a parallel promotion on a gambler's spree card (see "Gambler's Sprees" later in this chapter). When we tallied the expected return from both promotions, we were making more than $50 per hour.

Actually, for a time we were combining *three* promotions. Not only were we into the two promotions that paid cash, a third awarded prizes, such as keychains and T-shirts. Both Brad and I did this third promotion every day for 10 days, and we received 20 T-shirts from that casino.

Another time at another casino, we worked two promotions for five days. We had to play on under-100% machines, but we got back $800 in cash between the two promotions and slot club benefits, which more than covered all of our losses at the negative game. And as an added bonus, we took down six silk jackets.

Always look for opportunities to double up on promotions.

Positive Expectation, Yes — Guarantees, No

Because we play so many of them, we don't worry too much about losing money on any one promotion. We know that in the long run we'll come out ahead. But that's because we have the advantage (and the long-term) on our side. We look at it this way. If we participate in a good promotion enough times, it doesn't matter if we lose once in a while. Over the long haul, they'll produce a collective profit for us.

But if you go to casinos only once in a while, or visit a gambling town for only a few days, then a fair warning is in order. Playing a promotion, especially those that involve gambling coupons, might wind up costing you money. Coupons are enormously strong mathematically and you really should use them at every opportunity, but it's still possible to run into a dry stretch. If every time you use a coupon over a short trip you lose money, it can really do you in psychologically. You may never want to use a coupon again! But if you realize that the wins and losses of coupons and promotions should be considered collectively, over the long run, you'll continue to use them because you're sure to come out ahead in the end.

Even today, with as much experience as we have doing promotions and using coupons, we still get a little down if we make a special trip to a casino to use six or eight really good coupons and we end up losing. In the immortal words of one-time *Las Vegas Advisor* columnist, the Las Vegas Miser, "Coupons are evil things when you lose."

Promotions Come and Go

Caesars Palace used to give away free decks of used cards. It wasn't advertised anywhere, but if you knew about it, all you had to do was walk up to the cashier and ask for a deck. How did we know about the deal? In this case, we read about it in the *Las Vegas Advisor*. This is the sort of promotion that you find when you keep your eyes and ears wide open.

It's also the kind of promotion that's here today, gone tomorrow. One time you'll go to Caesars Palace and the cashier will smile and hand you a deck of cards. Then the next time she'll look at you like you're out of your mind (and swear that Caesars has *never* given away free cards). It happens all the time.

Almost all coupons and literature about promotions have a disclaimer written somewhere on them: "Offer may be changed or discontinued at any time at the discretion of management." Sometimes promos are shut down faster than you can say, "Oh well." It's just something you have to accept. We often phone in advance to double check on a promotion. This has saved us many wasted trips and much disappointment.

Promotions Checkerboard

Bonus Days for Slot Club Members

One of the best ongoing promotions at many casinos is double- and triple-point days for slot club members. Whatever the points are normally worth, on these days they're worth twice or three times as much. Bonus days for slot club members will probably put more cash in your pocket than any other category of promotion.

The Par-A-Dice in Peoria, IL, ran a promotion to celebrate the opening of the fourth deck on the riverboat. There's a Double Deuces game there that returns 99.6%. The slot club pays cashback of .28%, which is rather low. So Double Deuces plus regular slot club cashback returns 99.88%, still under our desired 100%. Double and triple points raise the payback to over 100%. But for this special fourth-deck promotion, the Par-A-Dice had quadruple points, which made the payback 100.74%. That's a very good return for a riverboat. (We also had a room comp.)

So look for extra-point times. Pay close attention to slot club mailings, especially their newsletters. This is another good reason to belong to as many slot clubs as you can: you might never consider playing at a particular casino because of its ordinary machines or minimal rebates, but out of the blue it may come up with a promotion that makes it worth your while to play there.

Game Bonuses

Always investigate placards and banners in both the table games and slot and video poker areas of the casinos. Often they're advertising bonus payoffs for particular hands. At the blackjack tables, for example, you might win a progressive jackpot if you're dealt three sevens, or a six-seven-eight in the suit of the day, or an ace of hearts and a jack of spades. Once in a while, a casino will pay 2-1 for natural blackjacks (the locals jump all over this valuable bonus and burn it out in a hurry).

Many casinos run special 4-of-a-kind bonuses at video poker; four queens pays double on Mother's Day, four kings pays double on Father's Day, four fours pays double on the Fourth of July, four fives pays double on Cinco de Mayo. Baldini's in Sparks (Reno's sister town) has been giving away six packs of Pepsi for 4-of-a-kinds for more than 15 years (it's Pepsi's largest account in all of Nevada). The Frontier used to put on a promotion in which you got a bonus when the first five or last five numbers of your social security number showed in a video poker hand.

The Sahara once ran a video poker promotion that was so fantastic it was a must-play for us. One day a week, they paid a $1,000 bonus on any royal flush. Not only that, but you could go for it on machines that were already over 100% return. It involved risk, because you could easily lose $700 or more on a quarter machine (and we did several times!). However, because the promotion ran for several months, we ended up solidly in the plus column.

It's important to know the math involved if you play these types of promotions. It helps to know the percentages when the payoffs on certain hands, like 4-of-a-kind or straight flush, are doubled. Computer experts can figure out the percentages easily; the rest of us can get the information in a book that gives these percentages. Knowing what they are will help you determine how good a promotion is. And again, don't forget to add in slot club points to find out what a promotion is really worth.

Slot machines are frequently the focus of game

bonuses. The last time we were in Tunica, MS, for example, three adjacent casinos (Sheraton, Horseshoe, and Circus Circus) all had big signs out front advertising double payouts for all hand-paid slot jackpots. The Four Queens in Las Vegas had a promotion where slot players got a card stamped for all hand-paid jackpots; when all the boxes on the card were stamped, the player got $100.

Although we like cash bonuses the best, many casinos give merchandise bonuses. Vegas Club ran a periodic promotion where they gave you a logo jacket for a royal flush in the suit of the day. Around Christmas, the El Cortez in downtown Las Vegas awarded boxes of candy for slot and video poker jackpots. One time the Mint (now Binion's) in downtown Las Vegas gave away real video poker machines to anyone who hit a royal!

Funbooks and Coupons

Funbooks are little coupon booklets handed out by the casinos; they're full of gambling, dining, and souvenir premiums and discounts. Always look for them. Ask at the slot club booth or welcome booth or casino cashier if the casino has a coupon book; you'll usually be asked to show out-of-state identification. Locals don't get to participate much in the funbook department, since the books are designed to attract out-of-state visitors into the casino.

The best casino funbooks are the ones that contain "lucky bucks." These are coupons for gambling that give you an extra dollar or two when you win an even-money bet. Lucky bucks generally come in 2-1, 3-2, and 7-5 denominations. Here's how they work. Make a $5 bet at a blackjack table (they can also be played at craps or roulette in most cases) and put down a 7-5 coupon with it. If you win, you're paid $7 instead of the normal $5. If you lay down a 7-5 coupon at a blackjack table and are dealt a natural, you'll be paid $7.50 for the natural (which returns 3-2) and given the extra $2 on top of that for a total win of $9.50.

Most lucky bucks come bound into the funbooks, but they're also given out loose as bonuses, perhaps when you attend a show or eat at a restaurant. When they're given away loose, they tend to find their way onto the floor or the tops of wastebaskets more easily. Look for them; they're valuable. How valuable? A 7-5 lucky buck is worth a little less than $1. It's calculated on the premise that you'll win close to half your hands. So the coupon is worth about half of the $2.

When you go to a show and the tables all have a 7-5 coupon on them, there's nothing wrong with picking up the coupons that people leave on the tables. Brad and I have come out of showrooms with fistfuls of lucky bucks. We wait until everyone else has filed out, then we go all around the room picking up coupons. We only leave when the help starts looking at us and it becomes too embarrassing to continue.

Some coupons specify that you can use only one per day. Others don't have any stipulations, so you can use them as many times as the casino will let you. There are gray areas in the use of coupons (see "Ethics and Gambling," pg. 187), so you'll have to make your own decision about how often you put down a coupon in the same casino.

One of the most valuable coupons you can get is one that substitutes for an ace at the blackjack table. Put the coupon down on the table with a bet and the dealer skips you the first time he deals around because you already have the coupon ace. If your next card is a 10 or a face card, you automatically have a blackjack. Otherwise you play the hand normally. There's risk here, because you have to bet your own money and the ace causes you to double down more. But an ace is the most powerful first card you can hold in blackjack. Starting with an ace as your first card, as you do with this coupon, gives you a 52% advantage—so multiply your bet by .52 to calculate your expected profit (about $2.60 for a $5 bet).

Another kind of lucky buck is called "matchplay." This is a coupon that doubles your payoff on even-money winners. Bet $10 of your own money in cash or chips along with a matchplay coupon. If you lose the hand, your $10 and the coupon are taken. If you win, you get paid $10 for your bet and an additional $10 for the coupon.

Matchplay is also worth a little less than half the face value of the coupon. A particular Las Vegas casino used to give out $5 matchplay coupons for each game—roulette, craps, and blackjack. With a set of coupons for each of us, worth about $14 ($30 in coupons divided by two minus the house edge), it made our daily walk to this casino quite worthwhile. One time we had umpteen sets of these coupons (thanks to our housekeeper) and the rules allowed us to use four sets per day. We didn't have a car at the time, but we didn't mind taking the round-trip (free) shuttle ride. We'll take two hours out of any day to collect our expected $56 in "pay."

Casinos aren't the only ones who hand out funbooks. When you travel to gambling destinations on air-room package deals, you'll usually be given special funbooks with coupons from many different casinos for food, merchandise, and gambling bonuses. Sometimes they're provided with your airfare; other times you pay a small fee ($20-$25) for an especially valuable coupon package. We buy these from our travel agent when we book our flight if we know they're worth more than they cost. Sometimes a travel agent will give you extra free funbooks if you ask.

Of course, the ultimate is getting the valuable travel-company coupons without paying for them ... from the maid. I cover befriending housekeepers in the "Long-Term" chapter, but it deserves emphasis. I have maids all over the place collecting unused coupon books that are left in rooms. I give the maids big tips — $10 or $20. And why not? I take these coupons and run them up to hundreds of dollars. This is a virtual gold mine.

Sometimes when you buy a gambling book, it'll have coupons in it. The *American Casino Guide* by Steve Bourie comes out once a year and has coupons in the back. It's published in Florida, so it has lots of deals from Mississippi. When you subscribe to *Casino Player* magazine, a bunch of coupons come with the deal, some for Vegas, some for the Caribbean, most for Atlantic City (where *Casino Player* is published).

Of course, the mother of all coupon books is the one you get when you subscribe to the *Las Vegas Advisor*. All the coupons are for Las Vegas casinos. If you use just two of the better coupons, you'll more than pay for the $50 subscription fee. It works out to getting the other 130 coupons, 12 issues of the newsletter, and access to the members-only sections of the *LVA* Web site for free. The newsletter isn't only valuable for its information, it also gives you a vicarious Las Vegas experience. Every month a little breath of Las Vegas air shows up in your mailbox.

Free Spins and Pulls

One of the most common promotions is a free spin of a wheel or a free play on a slot or video poker machine. These promotions are very common, but they usually don't pay off too well. Spin-the-wheel deals have been common in downtown Las Vegas; they've just been come-ons to get you into small slot joints, where you're pressured by expert hustlers to play the reel slots. But again, it doesn't cost anything, so it depends on how much time you have and if you can withstand the hard sell.

Once in a while a spin-the-wheel deal can be worth the effort. The free-play machine at Slots A Fun in Las Vegas, for instance, paid off in small increments but fairly frequently. Maybe once every 25 pulls someone won several quarters. Excalibur had a good free-pull promotion where we won caps, fanny packs, and keychains.

The best free play machine is in front of the Westward Ho, next to Slots A Fun. It's an on-and-off promotion, but when it's on everyone wins something. It's advertised as the world's largest slot machine, because the machine is hooked up to the casino's big marquee, which displays the cherries and bars. The grand prize is a car, but everyone who plays wins at least a painter's cap or a free drink. The Ho also gives away quite a few show tickets, probably because they have a little trouble filling up the showroom. Of course, to redeem the prizes you have to go inside, but that's all right. You don't have to gamble while you're there unless you want to.

Free Tournaments

If you have the time, one of the most fun and rewarding experiences you can have in Las Vegas is to play in one of the free daily tournaments. There's no risk involved and the potential rewards are great.

The Lady Luck in Las Vegas used to run a daily slot tournament and when we stayed downtown, we'd enter every day. We probably entered this tournament

25 or 30 times between us. It was a bit of a bother, because we had to get there and play, then come back a second time for the finals. But I won first prize ($500) once, which more than paid for the hours we spent hitting those spin buttons like mad.

A daily blackjack tournament at the Riviera was one of the best promotions in which we ever participated. There was no entry fee and you played with non-negotiable chips. The top two people from every table went to the finals where they had a shot at winning cash prizes. You were allowed to play morning and afternoon, so we played twice a day, every day, for many days in a row, but we weren't very lucky. We only got to the finals a couple of times, winning less than $50 each time. Although that didn't pay for our time, it didn't cost us anything out of pocket either.

However, a bonus attached to the tournament was lucrative for us. While playing, every time you got six cards without going over 21, you'd win 50 one-dollar "funny" chips. It actually turned out to be more valuable to get these non-negotiable chips than it was to get into the finals. We quickly learned to alter basic strategy to account for this unusual rule. You had to do some pretty strange things. For example, if you had a five-card 17, 18, or 19, you'd take a sixth card to try for the $50 in chips.

Not everyone tried for the six-card play, because they didn't realize how valuable the 50-chip bonus was. They thought the value was in trying to win the tournament. Had they paid attention to what we and some of the other informed players were doing, they would have known differently. Sometimes you can get good information on how to play a special promotion by watching what other people are doing. Look for the pros or well-informed locals who are doing it right.

Participating in this tournament involved some

complex logistics. We had to go to the Riviera twice a day, which was a hassle because we weren't staying there at the time. Sometimes we had to go back a third time for the finals. We had to be there at the right times to register both in the morning and the afternoon. When they discontinued the tournament, we had $2,000 in funny money and made around $1,400 in real money playing them at the regular casino games. Added to the $100 we won at the finals, our total profit after about three weeks of play was $1,500. We were glad we "bothered" with this promotion.

Fee Tournaments

When a tournament has an entry fee, you have to do some calculations. The thing you're calculating is called "equity"; you're figuring out whether or not the casino is giving back all the entry-fee money. If all the entry fees are not returned as prizes, then the tournament has negative equity. The casino has to return all the entry money, and give some extras such as free meals or rooms or parties, for it to be a positive-equity situation.

You also have to factor in whether playing the tournament is worth your time—again, daily tournaments can be time-consuming. We usually don't enter tournaments that have entry fees, although we know plenty of people who do and are very successful playing them.

Equity in tournaments that last several days tends to be high, because there are lots of tangible and intangible benefits. You may get three or four nights free, all your food, a welcome party, an awards banquet, and premium gifts such as jackets, jewelry, or luggage. In addition, the casino often returns all or almost all the entry fees as prizes.

Tournaments are also fun, and the competition is very friendly. So another thing you get is camaraderie: regular players on the tournament circuit get to be very friendly with each other and the tournaments are like little reunions.

You might wonder how the casino can hold tournaments where they give back more in prizes and comps than they take in. The casino holds positive-equity tournaments for the same reason that it has positive-expectation promotions. They're counting on people to play the regular games and machines when they're not involved in the tournament, which takes up only a small part of the three or four days that it runs.

In Atlantic City, the sponsors of a gambling festival ran a free slot tournament with prizes worth $40,000 that were paid by the festival host, the Taj Mahal. Meanwhile, the Taj gave a slot club card to every registered participant. It might seem impossible, but word was those slot cards generated a million dollars in win for the casino. Obviously, the million the Taj took in from these people when they weren't at the festival or playing in the tournament more than made up for what they gave away.

Playing slot tournaments requires no skill whatsoever, if everyone starts with the same number of credits and speed is not a factor. However, most tournaments are set up on a timed basis, so it takes some manual dexterity and mental concentration to stay on that spin button the whole time, usually 10 minutes. Sometimes getting just a couple more spins in than everyone else will give you a better shot at accumulating more points to win a bigger prize. You have to pay attention to when your credits have finished clicking on the meter; until the credits stop adding up, you can't spin the reels again. The object is to spin the reels as often as you can to give you the best shot at accruing the most points.

I'm always amazed at how many people sit in front of their machines in a daze long after the machine is ready to go again, or waste time celebrating a jackpot—either their own or their neighbor's. You've got to jump on that spin button as soon as the reels will turn.

Video poker tournaments, however, do require some skill. It used to be that the speed of play was the primary factor: you had a certain amount of time to play and the participants who could play faster had an advantage. These days the speed factor isn't as important as it used to be, since most tournaments are structured so everyone gets the same number of hands and even an average player can finish up in the allotted time. Under this arrangement, people who know the correct strategies have a slight advantage over those who don't (and the correct strategy for a video poker tournament might not be the same as the strategy for the same machine during regular play). But skill still isn't as important in tournaments as it is playing regular video poker, because tournaments are short term and anything can happen in the short term.

A number of casinos run weekly, or even daily, video poker tournaments that you have to pay money to enter, but all the entry money is returned in prizes. There's risk involved, but here there's no casino edge. One of the best of these took place at the Las Vegas Hilton. As soon as you paid the $25 entry fee, you were given a T-shirt and a free buffet (nearly returning the cost of entering). Since Hilton returned all the entry fees, the players had positive equity. But that wasn't all. While you were waiting for your turn to play, or for the finals, you could play the regular machines on the floor; every time you hit 4-of-a-kind, you got to spin a wheel or draw a ping-pong ball for more cash prizes. This promotion had so many good things about it that you could set your clock by us being at the Las Vegas

Hilton every Thursday night ponying up our $25 each to play, eating our buffet, getting our T-shirt, and hitting the over 100% video poker machines hard in the interim. Even if we knew we weren't in the finals, we always played right up until finals time, because we knew that every 4-of-a-kind we hit gave us another shot at extra cash. Brad won the tournament twice and got two $1,000 first prizes. I won $500 once.

I confess we cried a little when they discontinued the Hilton tournament. But that's the nature of casino promotions. I know of no promotion that was running when we first got to Las Vegas in 1984 that's still running today. The VIP Vacation package at the old Vegas World (now Stratosphere) went on for at least ten years, and it only stopped when Vegas World closed down so that Stratosphere could be built in its place. That was the longest large-scale promotion that I'm familiar with in Las Vegas.

Gambler's Sprees

Sprees come and go; I haven't seen one around for a while. But they're good promotions when they run. These programs are sometimes for table players, sometimes for machine players, and we've been on a few that allowed us to combine blackjack and video poker play. You pay a set amount of money to a travel agent in your home city for a spree package that can include any combination of airfare, hotel accommodations, food, shows, and matchplay chips. To qualify, you're required to play the table games a prescribed number of hours (or accrue a certain number of points if you're a slot or video poker player). After qualifying, you get a rebate on part of your original purchase price in some combination of cash and chips.

You have to compare the cost of the spree to what

you would pay for airfare, room, and food if you just booked it all on your own. We didn't participate in these sprees for very long, because we soon got our airfare cheap, sometimes even free (see "The Bump," pg. 143). And we soon didn't have to pay for rooms or food anyway because we were earning comps. Also, we were staying for such long periods of time that we were not looking for a program that lasted only three or four days. But for a couple (the programs are usually based on double occupancy) that comes to Vegas for only a few days at a time, sprees are often worthwhile.

Souvenirs and Stuff

I define "stuff" as anything the casino gives you that's not money. For example, the Riviera and the Four Queens had a program where you paid $20 up front and got 40 plays on a promotional slot machine. In rare cases you won $40 on these set-very-tight promo machines; if not, you got to choose a prize from their showcase. Most would cost you more than $20 if you went to a gift shop to buy them—logo items, cassette recorders, video casino games like blackjack and video poker—so it was a good deal.

You can also get a lot of good souvenirs, like T-shirts and sweatshirts and hats, by making race and sports bets. Read the sports section of the daily newspapers to see who has a promotion going. You won't necessarily want to make a bet just to get the souvenirs, but if you'd planned to place a bet on a team or a horse anyway, it's often worth your while to shop around. The best time of year to do this is the week before the Super Bowl. At that time, if we want to bet $100, we might bet $20 at five different casinos, or five different times in the same casino, because they're giving away souvenirs when you make a $20 bet. You learn how to work these promotions. Sometimes there's a limit of one or two per person; in that case Brad and I each do the maximum amount they allow.

Free photos are popular souvenirs. We have a whole album of them—with the "royal court" at Caesars in Atlantic City, with Bobby Berosini's orangutans at the Stardust in Las Vegas, in front of a hundred $10,000 bills at the Horseshoe, with casino mascots at the "lucky" video poker machines where we've hit big jackpots. These photos provide great memories of thrills we've had during our trips. (They do, however, keep us aware that although casinos are fun, they don't keep us from aging!)

Silverton used to have a promotion where you got a photo taken of you in Wild West costumes; it was free but you needed an out-of-state ID. You'd pay $15 or more in a typical touristy area for an old-time photo like this one. Brad and I had a blast doing it, living out some of our fantasies: sometimes I was a sexy barmaid and he got to be a cowboy; other times I was a Southern Belle and he got to be a Rebel general.

More often than not, casino funbooks have coupons for free souvenirs. Usually they're just chintzy keychains or caps. But not always. The Hard Rock casino gave out a funbook with a coupon for a free logo shot glass. It was a pretty blue, very different than the usual shot glass, and sold for around $5 in the gift shop. The Sands, before it closed, gave away several million logo mugs. We know many people who stocked their coffee-cup cupboards (and their friends' and neighbors' and family's cupboards as well) with Sands mugs.

If your stay in Vegas is limited, you probably don't have the time to run around hunting for the best free souvenirs. During our long stays, we eventually hit every casino that was giving out free things. We quickly learned which souvenirs are valuable and where to go back time after time and year after year. We also learned where not to bother returning. Sometimes we get a surprise: a casino that had good souvenirs in the past reverts to chintzy keychains, or someplace that's never excelled in the souvenir department suddenly starts giving away something good. You have to keep watching.

Food and Drink Deals

Food and drink coupons abound — total freebies, two-for-ones, and other money-off discounts. They show up regularly in the newspapers and the freebie magazines. Almost every funbook has at least one free-drink offer. Of course, you can get free drinks when you're playing, but it's nice to get them when you don't want to play, like when you just want to sit at the bar or in the lounge and relax a bit. The Boardwalk in Las Vegas once had an especially good funbook if you were looking for discounts and freebies in the food department. We enjoyed free ice cream, free hamburgers, and free all-you-can-eat pancake breakfasts.

For a long time, the Plaza funbook had a coupon for a free breakfast. What was really unusual about this breakfast coupon was that you could use it 24 hours a day. Also, the gratuity was included; you usually have to tip out of pocket when you use free coupons for food. Almost all of them say, "gratuity not included."

The Flamingo Las Vegas sometimes puts out a coupon for a free drink with a stub that you give the cocktail waitress. The casino picks up both the tab and the gratuity. This is our idea of a really good coupon, because tips are the one thing that you rarely get comped, and tips are one of our biggest expenses when we travel to gambling destinations.

Check Cashing

One of the strongest locals-only promotions in Las Vegas is related to the cashing of paychecks. Some of the "locals casinos" in the neighborhoods and outlying areas of town have excellent check-cashing incentives where the prizes can be very big: a Hawaiian vacation, a truck or car, even large monetary prizes.

Some casinos will give you a bonus for cashing government or pension checks; you just have to check on the requirements. Other casinos will give you a little something if you cash traveler's checks. Whenever you cash a check, ask if you get something for it.

Locals and Senior Citizens

Some promotions, such as check cashing, are geared specifically for locals. By showing a Nevada driver's license, you can get a discount on admission into Circus Circus' Adventuredome. Casinos in the outlying parts of Las Vegas cater more to locals, making them more likely to get mailings from those casinos than people from out of town.

Locals can sometimes get discounted show tickets, especially in December when business is slowest. The daily newspapers are *the* source for bargains aimed at locals.

For a long time, casinos didn't offer discounts or special promotions to senior citizens. They claimed — rather lamely, I always thought — that their promotions and loss leaders, and even their prices in general, were so low that they couldn't be discounted further.

No longer! Now casinos promote to senior-citizens big time; discounts are as common in casinos as they are in all other businesses. Many have a slot club-within-the-slot club with special cards for the over-55 set. Some have special prices for attractions and meals;

a few even have particular times when senior citizens actually eat free. Others put on events, such as exercise classes, investment seminars, and mini-Elderhostels for geezers like us. If you're over 55, keep your eyes peeled for promotions that'll save you money and improve your quality of life.

Show and Activity Discounts

I really don't like to pay for anything, but there are some things that you just can't get free. For those we settle for discounts. The local newspapers and the freebie mags are the best places to find show discounts. If a show is struggling, the casino will often advertise two-for-one coupons. Around Christmas a lot of shows are dark, but if they're not, the crowds are kind of thin. So the December holidays are a good time to find show discounts, some geared toward locals, others for anyone.

One time Brad wanted to see the Debbie Reynolds' Hollywood memorabilia museum (now gone), so I went through the freebie magazines. I found some two-for-ones, but they didn't work for us because I had no interest in going. I finally found a $2-off coupon and felt better about the whole thing. The moral? Never go to a show, a museum, or a special event without leafing through the dailies and freebie mags to see if there's a discount.

Never pay a thing to get into the Imperial Palace Auto Collection; look for free-admission coupons in racks and funbooks and in front of the Imperial Palace, handed out by leafleteers.

Promotions Out of the Blue

Sometimes an offer will show up in your mailbox and you'll have no idea how it got there. This happened to us a few years ago with a mailing from the Flamingo. We'd never played there, but Brad and I each got an invitation to stay three nights free in December. All we could figure was that at some time we must have signed up for something. This is why you should *always* sign up for everything. Who knows? You might get six day's worth of lodging for nothing.

Sometimes you plan to do promotions; other times you just bump into them. One day we were walking by the Aladdin and a man was handing out flyers advertising a promo in which participants rolled special dice to win prizes. We went in and Brad took his turn. He rolled a seven and won a pair of dice. Since we collect dice, that was a nice little prize for us. I took my turn and shot snake eyes, so I got another throw to win better stuff from a more valuable schedule of gifts. I wound up with a free T-shirt from the gift shop. Neither the dice nor the T-shirt cost us a thing.

Though we'd only played about four or five hours total in two different sessions at the Empress Riverboat in Joliet, IL, and only on 25¢ video poker machines, when they opened a new hotel we received a coupon in the mail for a free night.

The Stratosphere once sent Brad an invitation for two nights free plus $75 in cash. When I called up to make a reservation, I told the agent that Brad and I had stayed at Vegas World many times, and asked if they got our names from when we'd stayed there previously. "No, that's not the list we're using. We're using the list from hosts who used to work at other hotels," the agent replied. So if you get an offer from a casino where you've never played, maybe there's an employee in the promotions department who brought a mailing list with him from somewhere else. Casino personnel move around a lot, and they evidently take not only their high-roller lists, but their low-roller lists, too.

Is The Promotion
Train Slowing Down?

When a great promotion ends, I sometimes hear people complain that the promotions situation in that particular gambling destination is going downhill, and that soon there won't be any good deals left. Au contraire! My feeling is that promotions are getting better all the time. Competition is what drives casinos to offer better promotions, and there's more competition between casinos now than ever before. We're in the Golden Age of Promotions.

In Las Vegas especially, the megaresorts are forcing the smaller casinos to scramble. But it's by no means limited to Las Vegas. On a trip to Tunica, MS, just after the opening of Grand Casino, we saw promotions all over the place. The Grand is so big that the other Tunica casinos had to up the ante just to keep their customers. Three places were paying double jackpots and one gave away free buffets for one whole day. (Believe it or not, we didn't eat there because the lines were too long!)

For several years, there were less than half a dozen casinos in the Chicago area. But then Indiana added three riverboats in the Gary-Hammond area, which is just as close to Chicago as Elgin or Joliet. The mailings I got from the Empress in Joliet touted better-paying video poker machines and many more promotions. I couldn't wait until the Cincinnati-area riverboats opened! Hurray for competition!

8

The Bump
Airline Comps

It isn't just casinos that want to give you comps. Airlines can be just as generous with their "gifts." If you fly to your favorite gambling destination, then this section is for you.

Once many years ago, while sitting in a Vegas-bound plane waiting to take off, a flight attendant got on the PA and announced that anyone willing to catch a later flight would get dinner for two in a nice restaurant, $150 in cash, and a free round-trip ticket to anywhere in the United States. I looked at Brad and he looked at me and we wondered what it was all about; we'd never heard of this kind of thing before. But by the time we'd discussed it and decided to ask about the details, there were already takers. Later, I asked the flight attendant to explain the offer. That was the first time I heard the all-powerful word "bump." Since then we've been able to travel free all over the world more times than you might believe, just by taking advantage of that magic word.

The next time a flight attendant asked for volunteers to take a later flight, our hands were the first ones up. Why not? We weren't in any hurry. We were retired, so we didn't have any important business to attend to when we reached our destination. No one was waiting to pick us up.

We continued to volunteer at every opportunity. Sometimes we were selected to be bumped, other times they chose people who were closer to the front of the plane. I figured that there must be a way to ensure that if there was any bumping to be done, we'd be the bumpees. I began talking to reservation clerks, gate agents, and flight attendants. Soon I had all of the important details about the whole procedure. Gradually, down through the years, I've learned most, if not all, of the little secrets of the bump system. And now you'll learn them too.

Why It Works

Simply stated, the airlines often book more people on a flight than they have seats to put them in. They figure a certain percentage of passengers won't show up. Usually, that's what happens and there are enough seats to go around. People's plans change at the last minute. Businessmen make reservations on three or four flights because they don't know when their meetings will be over. Or maybe a couple is having such a good time on their vacation that they decide to stay another few days. In a gambling city, it might be a matter of someone being in the middle of a hot roll at the crap table and refusing to leave.

However, when everyone does show up for a particular flight, then some passengers will have to be bumped. Government regulations state that the airline must compensate passengers who cannot get a seat on an airplane for which they have a confirmed reservation. These are people who check in on time, but all the seats have been assigned. The gate agents are instructed to ask for volunteers to give up seats on the overbooked flight in return for some compensation. The bump works well for everyone. The passengers with confirmed reservations are happy, because they have to be on that first plane. The bumpees are happy, because they get some valuable comps. And the airline is happy, because now it has willing volunteers instead of unhappy passengers.

It's rare, but involuntary bumping does happen, when no one will volunteer to give up his seat. In these cases, the airlines have to pay big money to the people who get bumped against their will.

Planning To Get Bumped

If you're not properly prepared, getting bumped can be a nuisance or worse. But if you're ready as well as willing, then doing the bump is not only profitable, it can be an adventure.

First and foremost, you must have flexible travel plans. If you have to be back at work, or your arrival time impacts someone else's schedule, or if your trip is short, it's not worth it to be bumped. Bumping is strictly for people who have plenty of time on their hands. If that's you, there are ways to improve your chances of becoming a bumpee.

When you make your reservations, try to make them for a date and time when you think the airline will be busiest. Begin with holidays. You've seen the news stories about the day before Christmas or the day after New Year's; it's wall-to-wall people at the airports. Holidays are prime bumping times. Whenever you can book a flight around a holiday, do it.

However, don't book a flight specifically for a busy

time if you'll have to pay more for it. You won't always get bumped, and the times you don't you'll be stuck with the high fare.

Personally, I would never book a flight just to get bumped, but some people do. They pay the higher fare and hope for the best. I've heard of people who've gotten bumped three or four times on one day, just before Christmas — still, I've never felt it was a good gamble. If you want to get a cheap rate close to the holidays, you need to book it very far in advance. The earlier you book, the greater the possibility that there'll be low-fare seats available.

The busiest times are not just national holidays. Watch for regional events that create crowded conditions at your local airport: before and after the Kentucky Derby in Louisville, before and after the Indy 500 in Indianapolis, and the like. If you know where the Super Bowl and NCAA Final Four are being played a year in advance and coordinate coming and going from those particular cities when everyone else wants to, you're almost sure to be bumped.

If your home airport is small or you use smaller airlines, you may feel that you don't have very good bumping opportunities. Not true. Every airport has *some* busy times; you just have to identify them. And some of the niche airlines, because of their lower profit margins, overbook more frequently than the giants.

Let's talk specifically about flying to and from Vegas. Since this is where Brad and I fly to and from the most, it's also where we get bumped off airplanes the most. We have it down to a science. A lot of people go to Vegas for the weekend, so the best times to get bumped flying in are Friday afternoons and evenings; likewise, the best times to fly out are on Sunday afternoons and evenings. Even better is trying to hit any three-day holiday weekend. Christmas, New Year's, Memorial Day, Fourth of July, and Labor Day are pretty safe bets for crowded aircraft. We've had great success making reservations on overbooked planes at these times.

Before and after big conventions and gambling events are also good times to book your flights. Comdex, the Super Bowl, the Final Four, the NBA playoffs, and the last couple games of the World Series are all very busy times in Las Vegas. A few winters when we only stayed until the end of January, we always booked a flight out of Vegas on the Monday after the Super Bowl. We got bumped every year because those flights were always overbooked.

You can increase your chances of getting bumped by avoiding direct or non-stop flights. Routes that involve connecting flights are better because they afford two chances to get bumped. Actually, this is better than double the odds: connecting cities tend to be hubs and your chances of being bumped in a hub are always greater.

Also, don't fly by charter. Charters do not overbook, so they don't bump. If you take a charter, you've got no shot.

"B" Day Arrives

To improve your odds of getting bumped, show up at the airport very early—an hour and a half or so before flight time. You want to be one of the first people to check in. When you check your luggage at the ticket counter, ask if the flight is overbooked. The ticket agent will tell you whether it is or isn't. If it's not overbooked at that time, don't give up hope, but it's less likely that you're in a bumping situation.

If the plane is overbooked, or so crowded there's a chance that it will be by flight time, tell the ticket agent you'd like to leave your name as a volunteer to be bumped. This is a powerful strategy. Sometimes your name will be entered in the computer on the spot. This means that the airline has already started the volunteer list and yours is the first name on it. If the flight is almost full, but not quite overbooked, ask the agent to start the volunteer list, just in case. Be nice, but impress upon her how anxious you are to get your name in the computer. In any case, the agent will still give you tickets with seat assignments like everyone else. An overbooked plane is not a concern at the ticket counter. Even after the seats run out, the ticket agents continue to check people in and handle their luggage. The only difference is passengers are told to get their seat assignments at the gate desk.

Some airlines don't log volunteer lists in their computers. In that case, you'll be told to go up to the gate and give your name to the check-in agent. Here too, it's good to be early at the gate. I'm usually there before the agent even opens the desk, which is 45 minutes to an hour before the flight. I always try to be the first person in line.

As soon as the gate agent shows up, I ask if the flight is overbooked. If she says that the plane is not even close to being full, end of story. If she says that it may be a little overbooked, I tell her that I wouldn't mind volunteering, "just in case you need to bump a couple of passengers," I might say. I ask if she wants to keep my ticket. If there's any chance that someone will need to be bumped, the agent will take the ticket right then and hold it. It's always a good sign when the gate agent takes your ticket, especially if you're first in line. It means *your* seats will be given to someone else with reservations if the plane is overbooked.

We're very nice to those gate agents. I mean it: we're luvvy-duvvy. I tell you those gate agents adore us—especially compared to people who have to be back at work on Monday and are in jeopardy of being involuntarily bumped from the plane on Sunday night. We've seen it many times. These people get unbelievably nasty, even menacing. This can make a gate agent's life pretty miserable. In fact, gate agents lives are generally miserable even if they don't have to bump people involuntarily. They work on the firing line and almost always have to deal with impatient people who are having some sort of problem. Then here we come, telling them that we don't care about getting on this particular airplane. We don't care when we get to where we're going. We'd like to do them a big favor. They can give us the seats that are most convenient for them. They love us. Don't feel embarrassed about volunteering. If you want to be really popular at the airport, volunteer to be a bumpee.

Just because the gate agent holds your ticket, being bumped is not a certainty. I usually loiter near the desk so I can eavesdrop on what the gate agents are saying to one another. I watch the line to see if it stops moving because the plane is full and they can't assign any more seats.

The Most Exciting Ten Minutes in an Airport

The critical time is 10 minutes before scheduled take-off. On domestic flights, in order to claim your seat, you're required to appear at the gate at least 10 minutes before the plane is scheduled to depart (on international flights it's 30 minutes). The gate agents can't give away confirmed-reservation seats until then. The people who've been sent upstairs from the ticket counter with reservations but no seats will get assignments that become available in the last ten minutes.

What happens if, after everyone with reservations is on the plane, there are still two seats vacant (even though they aren't your original seats)? The gate agent will thank you, give you your tickets back, and direct you onto the plane. Does this mean you haven't been bumped? Not at all. At that point, a variety of things can still occur. One thing that can happen is you're given two seats together and you're on your way.

The worst is that you get split up. The gate agent may have already given away your adjoining seats and you wind up filling single seats. This is a minor inconvenience. Often you'll be able to switch with someone nearby so you can sit together.

Another thing that's happened to us many times is we get put into first class. We give up our coach seats to some desperate last-minute arrival and we get ushered into the front of the plane where they have a couple of extra spots. We get to drink free liquor if we want, eat gourmet meals, have plenty of elbow room, and smile because we got upgraded—just for being nice. When you're in first class, particularly on a flight to Las Vegas, everyone looks at you like you're high rollers. Little do they realize that we're dyed-in-the-wool low rollers and not only didn't we have to pay to be in first class, we probably didn't pay for our coach seats either (as you'll later learn). This is a classic case of low rollers looking like high rollers.

One time we volunteered in New York to be bumped off a flight to Europe. Right up to the last minute we thought we would be bumped, but ultimately we weren't. Still, we were put in business class, which is a luxurious upgrade, one that's much appreciated on such a long flight: there's lots of leg room, nice reclining seats, and they even give you slippers for your feet and eye masks so you can sleep. They serve gourmet food with wine and tablecloths on your tray. This was a red-eye and we were already tired, so we thought this was the greatest airplane ride we ever had. Just for volunteering.

One last thing can happen (and we've gone through this a couple of times). You get on the plane, you settle into your seats, and then your name is announced over the loudspeaker. Because of some last-second situation, you're called off the plane and two other people take your seats. This usually occurs when people with reservations show up just before the gate is locked and have a good excuse for being late (almost always because their connecting flight arrived just in the nick of time). It's always a thrill when it turns around and you do get bumped after already being on the plane.

When we get bumped, we're always the first, and sometimes the only, passengers to give up our seats. If the gate agents need more seats, occasionally other people have also signed up. What if they need more seats after they've gone through all of us eager beavers? That's when they come on the plane and start asking passengers to volunteer to get off. This is the second worst-case scenario for the airlines, because it can quickly turn into a bidding war if they have any trouble getting volunteers. They may have to offer a more generous incentive to entice people to postpone their travel plans. We never gamble and wait until they come on the plane to beg. We'd rather be first on the list than hope that they get desperate later and up the ante.

The absolute worst-case scenario for the airlines is when they can't get anyone to give up a seat and they have to delay ticketed passengers. Involuntarily bumped passengers can cause the airlines enormous grief.

Collecting Your Just Rewards

The sweetest sound to our ears is the locking of that gate door to the jetway when we're still on the airport side. The plane finally flies off and we're still standing there at the gate. Now the fun begins! First, the gate personnel tell the bumpees when the next plane is leaving. It's usually no longer than three or four hours later, though if the hour is already late, the next flight might not depart till morning. Whenever it leaves, the gate agent will usually book you on the next flight. This is also a good time to have your bump antenna on alert. The next plane might also be full, so you can make the same play again. Or it may be full on coach, but first-class seats are available, which they'll give you freely.

Then it's time to work out the details of payment. What will the airlines give you when you get bumped? This varies from airline to airline. It also varies within the airline, depending on how long you have to wait before the next flight leaves and how long the flight itself is. If you get bumped from a one-hour shuttle, you won't get as much as you would on a five-hour cross-country flight.

Twenty-one years ago when we started getting bumped, we frequently flew on TWA. Every time we got bumped in Vegas, they gave us each $400 in TWA airfare credit. At that time it cost $200 for a round-trip ticket from our Midwest home. The credit was enough to cover our next two trips. Nowadays, the typical amount runs from $100 to $300. Few airlines give you actual cash; instead they give you airline scrip, or "transportation vouchers," to use when you buy your next ticket. The next time you want to fly, you find the cheapest flight you can so your voucher will take you as far as possible. Some airlines give you change back from the voucher. Others don't; in that case you should only use it when the cost of your next flight is more than the amount of the voucher (you make up the difference in cash).

Some airlines don't use scrip and instead give you a free ticket to anywhere in the U.S. that the airline flies. These tickets are extra valuable when you use them on flights that are more expensive than the one from which you got bumped. You don't have a choice in the matter: some airlines pay off in scrip, others in tickets. (A fine point. If you're given a free flight to anywhere in the U.S., you don't earn frequent-flier miles on it. That's why we prefer to fly on airlines that give you airline scrip; tickets you "buy" with these vouchers *do* earn frequent-flyer points.)

If you don't plan to fly again for several years, getting bumped might not do you much good. The vouchers are usually only good for up to one year. The tickets do have various restrictions, such as when you can use them (blackout dates are often around holidays). Some vouchers and tickets are nontransferable, while others can be given to another person. The airlines expressly forbid selling free vouchers, tickets, or frequent-flier miles, although it is commonly done. But if you're like us, we'll be flying again in another month or two, so we can always use airline credit or actual tickets. It's the same as money in our pocket.

Sometimes you can negotiate your bump payment. It does vary and the gate agent often seems to have a bit of latitude. If she says she'll give us $100, I say, "Oh? We got a hundred and fifty last time. Couldn't you give us the same?" Polite requests have worked for us on many occasions.

If the flight doesn't take off for several hours, you should also be offered scrip for food. In most cases, though, the gate agents are too busy to think about feeding you. So just like in the casino, I ask for it. I've never been refused. No one expects you to sit in the airport and starve; nor do they expect you to use your own money. The airline will give you enough credit to enjoy a meal; you can use it in any airport restaurant, from Taco Bell to the bar and grill.

You can also ask to use the phone to make alternate arrangements because of the delay. Often they'll even dial the number for you. Voila! A free-long-distance phone call.

On the other hand, you'll never have to ask for room comps. If the next flight doesn't take off till the next day, the airline will automatically make arrangements for you to spend the night at a hotel near the airport (see "Overnight Bumps" below).

Sometimes the bumping doesn't go so smoothly. Maybe the wait turns out to be a little longer than you were told. Maybe you don't get quite as large a reward as you wanted. Don't expect the moon—take what they give you, ask nicely for a little more, but if they can't give it up, don't fret about it. After all, this is free money. If you get $300 and have to wait three hours in the airport, that's $100 an hour! There aren't too many people that $100 an hour won't make at least a little happy.

Overnight Bumps

If you plan to volunteer to be a bumpee, you'll need to pack a little differently than usual. You should always carry an overnight bag with enough clothes and toiletries to last until you get to your destination. You might not be reunited with your luggage till the next day. (You never know until the last minute whether you'll be bumped, but your checked luggage is on your original plane winging its way to your destination with or without you.) As long as you're adequately prepared, staying overnight waiting for the next plane out can be an adventure. You're put up in a hotel or motel near the airport, to and from which you're transferred by free shuttle. These are always good accommodations—Holiday Inns, Airporter Inns, Sheratons, and the like. You're comped to dinner and breakfast. Since we don't like to wake up early, if they tell us the first flight is at 7 a.m., we'll ask for a later flight. We'll generally get on a 10 a.m. or noon flight and turn the overnight bump into a mini-vacation.

When you get to your destination, you have to go to the baggage office to collect your luggage, since it arrived on an earlier flight than you did.

People sometimes ask me, "Aren't you impatient to get to Las Vegas when you're bumped overnight?" My answer is always, "Of course." Even if we've been to Vegas four times that year, we're still always anxious to get there. But we also think about all the free trips we've taken, all over the world, thanks to getting bumped. So arriving in Las Vegas one day later, especially if we're going to be there for an extended stay, doesn't make any difference.

The Bump Express

Most of the time, you don't have to stay overnight when you get bumped. In fact, we've actually had the experience of getting bumped and arriving in Las Vegas earlier than our original flight! How is that possible? Well, sometimes the flight you get bumped off of connects in a busier city. The flight we miss might go through Chicago and get delayed, while the flight we catch goes through Dallas with no problems. We arrive in Las Vegas *before* our checked luggage. That's another reason to pack overnight carry-ons appropriately.

We've had such short waits between planes that by

the time the gate agent got the paperwork done, we just walked over to the other gate and got on that plane less than an hour later. Usually you fly on the next plane of the same airline, but sometimes they'll put you on another airline. We'll never forget an experience we had in New York on our way to Germany. The plane was full and we were bumped. We were told that we could get to our destination only a couple of hours later than originally scheduled if we were willing to take two seats on the Kuwait airline, which had just resumed service after the Gulf War.

When we went over to the Kuwait waiting area, everyone there looked like someone Sadaam Hussein didn't like. All the women were veiled and everyone was wearing somber colors, while we were in bright sweatsuits. Though I was a bit nervous, it turned out to be a memorable experience. We had one of the best meals we've ever eaten on an airplane and we made it quite safely to our destination only a couple of hours after our original flight.

Bumps on Bumps

You can get bumped more than once for the same trip. One time in Chicago, our plane was full, we got bumped, and were each paid $150 in vouchers. The next flight was just an hour later, but when we got to that gate, the agent told us that that flight was full, too. So we immediately volunteered to be put on the list again. We got bumped the second time and got more vouchers. We actually almost got bumped a third time that day. (I've heard the story of one family of six that got bumped five times the day before Thanksgiving and got enough airline scrip for a trip around the world — for all six of them!)

Talk about double-dipping! What was funny about

our two bumps in Chicago is that the original flight had
been free. We'd acquired the ticket with airline scrip
from a previous bump.

Which goes to show that you can be bumped off a
flight that you paid for with bump money or frequent-
flier miles. When you're bumped it doesn't matter what
kind of ticket it is. Well, sometimes it matters a little bit.
One time we were going to London from New York on
a frequent-flier free ticket and we got bumped, along
with several other passengers. We didn't get quite
as much scrip as the bumpees who'd paid full fare. I
questioned the ticket agent about it. (I never just leave
anything to chance; maybe she'd made a mistake …). I
asked nicely and I was told that that particular airline's
policy was to reduce the scrip payment if you were
using frequent-flier miles. But that's the only time it's
ever made a difference.

Frequent-Flier Fun

Remember our favorite word, "free"? My favorite
phrase is "frequent flier." The frequent-flier situation
is another story altogether. I could write a book about
it. Suffice it to say, it's a complicated subject and you
have to know the rules inside and out. Every airline
has a frequent-flier club with its own system and strategies. You have to read all the literature they send you
very carefully; a lot of the relevant information is in
the fine print. But these clubs have given us thousands
of dollars worth of flights over the years.

The basics are very much like slot clubs. (Riding on
a plane and not accruing frequent-flier miles is an even
worse sin than playing video poker and not having a
slot club card in the card reader.) You should always,
even if you don't think you'll ever fly on that airline
again, join the frequent-flier club before you take the

flight. You never know what they'll send you in the mail; the newsletters are full of money-saving offers. We've gotten bonus miles for filling out surveys, getting someone else to join, and renting from car companies or staying at hotels that are partners with the airline.

Just like with the slot clubs, we try to patronize one core airline at a time, and then pick up a second. Since benefits do expire on most airlines, we try not to have any more than two airlines at a time on which we're accumulating frequent-flier miles.

Always give your frequent-flier number when you make your reservations and be sure you're credited for the flight when you check in. This often doesn't happen automatically. We always give our frequent-flier number even if we're flying on a frequent-flier free ticket. The rule is you're not supposed to accrue miles on frequent-flier miles. But we always give them our number and lots of times they'll give us free miles for that trip anyway.

We accrue frequent-flier miles in lots of ways besides just flying and earning them. We look for promotions, just like we do at the casinos. We like to fly when they're giving double miles, just like double-point times at the slot club. Occasionally they even award triple miles.

We have a credit card that's linked to our frequent-flier clubs and we charge everything we can on it. Since we pay off the credit card every month, we avoid all interest charges. (If you don't pay off your credit card balance every month, this doesn't make sense, because you have to pay such a high interest rate that it wipes out the value of your frequent-flier benefits.)

The value of frequent-flier miles varies, depending on how you use them (long trips or short ones, for example), but I usually figure one cent per mile. So for every $1 we put on the credit card, we get a 1% advantage (with no risk). We charge all of our gas, groceries, airline tickets, restaurant meals, household purchases, and doctor bills. Every time we buy something, we're adding on miles to get free trips all over the world.

You can carry the credit card benefits a little further if you're very organized. Some airlines give you a two-for-one airline ticket when you first get their credit card. So one year we sign up for a credit card in one of our names and get our free companion-fare certificate. The next year we cancel that card and sign up in the other name and get another certificate. Even if you have to pay a yearly fee, $40-$60, a free airline ticket is worth much more than that. Then perhaps the third year we cancel the second credit card and find another airline that's having a free-ticket promotion and repeat the process. So we have a new credit card and a free airline ticket every year.

Happy flying. Maybe I'll see you at the gate putting your name on the volunteer list.

9

Long Term in Las Vegas
or
Having a Life

In early 1993, the *Las Vegas Advisor* ran a story about the Queen of Ku Pon staying in Las Vegas for 50 nights and only paying for one. A month later, a man wrote to the *Advisor*, commenting that staying for almost two months in Las Vegas hotel rooms sounded about as fun as having a root canal. His was a common response to our lifestyle. Often people looked at us sadly, as if they were thinking how uncomfortable, boring, even degenerate it was.

If you live in Las Vegas like we do now, you don't gamble 24 hours a day, seven days a week (not even if you're addicted!). Likewise, when we spent multiple weeks in Vegas, we didn't gamble round the clock. We shopped sales, telephoned our broker, took in a movie matinee, or went out dancing. If there was a good mini-series on, we'd watch the TV screen, not the video poker screen. The point is there are lots of other things to do in Vegas besides gamble. We refer to the time we spend in the casino world as our "artificial" life; all of the other activities are our "real" life.

Eating

One valuable and little-known amenity that made our long-term visits more comfortable when we stayed in hotels was a mini-refrigerator. We usually stayed at casinos that offered them for free and it was the first thing I asked for when I checked in. I told the front-desk clerk that I was on a special diet (which is true) and that I needed a fridge. Most of the time you won't even have to cite a special reason. Just ask for one and it will usually be supplied at no charge.

Sometimes you can get a room that already has a fridge in it. All you have to do is ask for one at check-in before the clerk has assigned your room. If they have one, it's yours. In Las Vegas, the Riviera, Westward Ho, Stardust, Lady Luck, and Frontier, among others, have rooms with built-in mini-refrigerators.

Otherwise, the desk clerk will call housekeeping, and usually by the time you get to the room, somebody has delivered the fridge on a hand truck. We always tip that person; it's pretty heavy.

Having a fridge in your room gives you a lot of options when it comes to eating. First of all, when your meals are comped, you can order up big time, knowing that you can store the leftovers; we find that most casinos slather so much food on you that no single human can eat it all in one sitting.

Eating three meals a day in restaurants is tough. It takes up too much time, especially when you have to wait in line to get in; also, you tend to overeat. No one who stays long-term in a casino destination should eat steak or bacon and eggs for breakfast every morning, not even if it's only 99¢, or even comped. Some people don't mind doing it; some even like it. You might *want* to do that for four days, or even 40, but your heart and arteries will thank you if you don't. We ate one meal (comped, of course) per day in a casino restaurant, and several small meals and snacks the rest of the time in our room. Occasionally, we stopped at a casino snack bar for a mini-meal or ate lunch at a fast-food place when we were out and about.

Every few days we went to the grocery store. Small stores are within walking distance of all the casinos; being a gambling town, big supermarkets within driving distance are open 24 hours. We'd load up on fruit, yogurt, cereal and milk, peanut butter and crackers, carrot sticks, juices and soft drinks — all the things that we like at home. Having food in your room saves you a lot of money and is also a healthier diet than eating in a restaurant three times a day.

Sleeping

Simply stated, we stay where we can get our rooms for free — that's the biggest consideration. There's a second consideration: avoiding having to move around excessively. Though we did in the early days, later on we never stayed anywhere for a single night; it was just too inconvenient, even if it was free. We did, occasionally, stay in a non-core casino for two or three nights when it brought something extra, like free show tickets, a free tournament, or other good promotions that required us to be checked into the hotel.

One thing we bumped up against once in a while was a state regulation that says you can only stay at a hotel-casino for 14 days. Allowing you to stay longer would classify the casino as a residential hotel, and that's a different licensing category. To circumvent the rule, having two names to use comes in handy. Brad and I having different last names was a huge benefit. We could stay 14 days under one of our names and 14 days under the other. Though we never tried it, I suppose we could have gone back to the first person's name and stayed 14 days; if the casino let us, we could have done it indefinitely.

I liked to stay two weeks at one hotel and then move, anyway. We switched from the Strip to downtown to provide variety. When you're staying at one casino you have a tendency to do things the same way. One of the things you want to guard against during long-term stays is boredom and getting in a rut. When you stay on the Strip for two weeks you do the Strip casinos and walks and shopping and activities. Then when you switch to downtown for two weeks, you do a different set of casinos, with different promotions, souvenirs, restaurants, and a general change of scenery.

Housekeeping

Every low roller needs a maid. In the promotions chapter I discussed how important it is to ask the maid to bring you discarded coupon books. Since we stayed in the same hotels often, we became friendly with several housekeepers who were happy to do this for us on a continuing basis. Every couple of months, whether we stayed in their section or not, we checked in with them and they usually had a big bag full of coupons waiting for us.

While we no longer regularly stay in Las Vegas hotels, I still like to become acquainted with the maid, not just for all the things she can do for me, but simply because she's a hard-working woman with a dirty job. Frequently, she's an immigrant from a country she had to flee for reasons of economics or safety or freedom. She's got kids and grandkids, heartaches and joys, just like the rest of us. Treating her with respect and generosity not only gets you what she can give you, but also gives you a good feeling just for having done so.

I always treat the housekeeper as a human being, unlike some people who think of her as a robotic servant. I call her by name, sympathize if she tells me her boyfriend dumped her, and rejoice if she tells me she has a new grandchild. I try to put myself in her position and find ways to make her job easier. We always pick up after ourselves and every other day or so I tell her it's her "day off" from our room. We hand her our dirty towels and get clean ones, and that's all it takes for her to get "credit" for cleaning our room.

Periodically, the maid does come in and change your sheets, vacuum, scrub the tub, and do some heavy-duty cleaning. In this case, we tip her. Not every time, but if we stay a week, for example, we may tip $5 or $10, depending on how nice she's been to us and how good a job she's done.

The housekeepers really appreciate our friendliness and cooperation. They not only ply us with extra Kleenex, toiletries, and the fluffiest towels, but they give us "leave-behinds" from other rooms — a bottle of wine, a fruit basket, magazines, and souvenirs.

Laundry

One thing that surprises me is that almost no casino has a laundry room for its guests. I suppose most people only stay two or three days and bring enough clothes so they don't have to waste their vacation time watching them go round and round in the dryer.

But if you stay for weeks or months at a time, you have to do your laundry. Of course, if you have a car, you can drive to the laundromat. If you don't have a car, you still have several options. Sometimes the maid will take home a sack of laundry to wash. We would agree on a price and get our laundry back clean the next day.

Wherever there's an RV park, there's always a laundromat that anyone can use: Silverton, Circus Circus on the Strip, and plenty of places on Boulder Highway.

If you're staying at a hotel and there are some residential apartments nearby, they'll have laundry rooms that often aren't locked. There may be a sign that says, "For the use of the residents only," but we've used them and no one ever asked us to leave. We put our quarters in the machines and cleaned up after ourselves and we didn't think anyone really minded.

For instance, at Sun Harbor Budget Suites behind the Stardust, there's a laundry room that's open most of the time and is not heavily used. We washed our clothes there and were never a bother to anyone.

The one thing you don't want to do is send your clothes out to the valet laundry service. I've looked at those price lists and it would be cheaper just to throw away your clothes and buy new ones than to pay the prices they charge. By the time you pay to have a pair of socks washed, you could buy a new pair at Kmart and come out ahead.

Getting Around

You've got plenty of options for getting around Las Vegas whether you stay long-term or short. You can walk. You can ride the city bus, known as CAT (for Citizens Area Transit), or you can catch the free casino shuttles. You can ride the Strip and downtown trolleys or catch taxi cabs. You can rent a car. Or you can bring your own car with you.

During our longer winter stays, we drove to Las Vegas and had our own car. Even though it was a long drive, it was worth it for us to have our own transportation. We could get around to all the casinos, play where there were good machines, put some points in our non-core slot club accounts, and take advantage of all the good promotions. Also, there was the psychological factor I've been talking about: having a car enables you to do other things besides gamble.

Most of the time, however, we didn't have our own vehicle because we flew in. Occasionally, we rented a car for a week, sometimes two. We generally did this during the hot summer months when it's oppressive to walk too far outside.

But in the non-summer months when we didn't have our own car, we walked and we rode CAT, the city buses. Las Vegas has a good public bus system. You can get anywhere on a bus, fairly conveniently and inexpensively. For Strip routes it's only $1 for senior citizens and kids and $2 for everyone else; it's 60¢ and $1.25, respectively, for off-Strip routes. There are also ways to do it even more cheaply by buying passes or tokens in quantity. We tried not to ride the Strip bus during rush hour on the Strip during the week, or on weekends, when the traffic is slow and the buses are packed (and there's a danger of getting pickpocketed). But on the whole, we found that riding the bus in Las Vegas is an efficient way to get around.

In addition to the municipal bus, many casinos have free shuttle buses that run around town. These are usually the off-Strip casinos, which pick up and drop off people in convenient Strip locations, such as at the Fashion Show Mall and MGM Grand.

Whether you have your own vehicle, rent a car, ride the buses and shuttles, or walk, the more you use them in your low-roller repertoire, the more mobility you'll have.

Gambling

We incorporate principles of real life into our gambling routine. On average, Brad and I combined play about eight hours of video poker a day (Brad puts in five hours to my three.) If we feel good and it's a double- or triple-point day, we might play video poker for eight hours each. Other days we don't go near a video poker machine. We find that when we take "real-life" breaks, time to smell the roses, we're much fresher when we come back to the gambling.

Whenever possible, Brad and I play together. Sitting side by side makes it easier for one of us to watch the other's machine during breaks. This comes in handy particularly if we're playing a promotion and all the good machines are taken. At those times, you don't want to leave your machine, because it'll be taken while you're gone. Hovering around the good promotions are what we call "vultures," people who get there a little late and chomp at the bit to grab your machine. If someone is watching it for you, you can ward them off.

On breaks, we go to the restroom, get a bite to eat, maybe even take a little trip to the gift shop. We often step outside to get away from the second-hand cigarette smoke that fills most casinos. I sometimes run up to my room and relax for 10 or 15 minutes.

Gamblers would play better if they took a break at least every couple of hours, particularly from blackjack or video poker where strategy and concentration are involved. Breaks recharge the body and refresh the mind, so you're less likely to make errors and more likely to play longer on a day that you're earning double points or taking advantage of a juicy promotion.

Avoiding Loneliness

Contrary to popular opinion, Las Vegas isn't a cold sterile place where everything is just gambling and business. It wouldn't have been possible for us to stay as long as we did in Las Vegas if we didn't make some friends along the way.

Several times a year, friends from around the country met us in Las Vegas. Even when we didn't live here, we had plenty of comps to treat them to dinner or a show. It was fun to show them the sights and teach them how to play video poker. A particular treat was when someone we knew decided to get married in Las Vegas, and then we got to join in the celebration.

Another thing we love to do is fly our grandchildren in (with or without their parents). There's no better way to see the family-friendly Las Vegas than with a family. Of course, you can do the volcano, the white tigers, and the dolphin pools at the Mirage; the pirate show at TI; the rides at Luxor; the talking statues at the Forum Shops at Caesars; the circus acts and midway games at Circus Circus; the midway, motion machine, and *Tournament of Kings* at Excalibur; and the dancing waters-and-laser show at Sam's Town on your own, but it's more fun to watch all these spectacles from a kid's point of view. These days there's so much for kids to do in Las Vegas that when our grandchildren are with us, we never lack for entertainment.

We take them to the top of the Stratosphere, Circus Circus' Adventuredome, the Masquerade parade at the Rio, and the Fremont Street Experience. For older children, there's the roller coasters at New York-New York and Buffalo Bill's. We also go to fun centers off the Strip where you can play miniature golf and ride bumper cars and boats.

A list of all the attractions in Las Vegas is found in the Friday *Las Vegas Review-Journal*, the morning daily newspaper. You should also pick up a good guidebook to Las Vegas for detailed descriptions of the non-gambling things to do; Deke Castleman's *Nevada Handbook* is a good one.

We met some of our best friends at a video poker machine. Years ago when we were learning Deuces Wild, we were sitting at a bank of machines at the Riviera. A couple was sitting beside us, and the woman said, "I see you're using a strategy card."

I said, "Yes, we're just learning how to play Deuces Wild."

She said, "I learned how to play using that same strategy chart."

Later that night we bumped into them again at another casino. We got to talking in earnest and realized that we had a lot in common. So we decided to compare our experiences at dinner at the coffee shop, where we both had comps. To make a long story short, they liked Las Vegas so well that they bought a condo here too — and we have been close friends ever since.

Staying Healthy

One of the most important things in our life is exercise. Vegas is a great place to walk — it's flat and there's always some new and interesting "trail." In the name of exercise and positive expectation, we often walk a couple of miles for one little promotion. We like to do some couponing on our walks, which makes them healthy for our bodies (exercise and fresh air), our minds (clear out the casino cobwebs), and our pocketbooks (coupons give you a big edge).

Most casinos have pools where you can stay cool in the water and get some good exercise at the same time. The best time to go if you want to swim laps is early in the morning when the pool first opens. After that, it can often be too crowded to swim for exercise without bumping into a bunch of splashers.

In addition to pools, most, if not all, of the large Strip and neighborhood hotels have health clubs or at least exercise rooms; some have extensive spas. When we stayed at the big Las Vegas hotels, we took health-club breaks every day. Best of all was getting comped to the health club through the slot club. When we lived in Indianapolis and decided to join a health club, we looked around for one that had at least one affiliate in Las Vegas; that way we didn't always have to stay in hotels with health clubs. We don't mind taking breaks from gambling to work out. You have to keep those muscles strong so you can play video poker machines for long periods!

Another thing we do is take walks in shopping malls. It's climate controlled, there's lots to look at, and the fast-food courts have salad bars and healthy options. If you're on the Strip, you can walk at the Fashion Show Mall or the Forum Shops at Caesars. If you have a car, you can drive to the Boulevard, Meadows, or Galleria malls located away from the Strip.

Having a refrigerator in the room helped us eat healthier. We didn't have to face a steady diet of casino buffets and snack bar hot dogs. We snacked on plenty of fruits and vegetables and other healthy fare.

We never had a medical emergency in Las Vegas before we lived here. If we had, we'd have called the hotel operator who would dial 911. Emergencies in casinos do happen frequently, as would be expected with tens of thousands of visitors concentrated on the Strip and downtown at any given time, many of them senior citizens. We see ambulances in front of casinos all the time and often joke to each other that "someone has OD'd on slot machines or buffets." However, sometimes it's sobering. We once watched a rescue squad work feverishly to revive a man who had slumped to the floor with a heart attack in a keno lounge—but they were unsuccessful. The incidence of coronaries in casinos is high, necessitating casino companies to buy defibrillators and train security personnel in their use.

What do you do if you're in need of non-emergency medical attention? The front desks of the hotels have a list of all the places nearby where you can get medical help. You can also look in the Yellow Pages and find walk-in clinics or even doctors who will come to your hotel room. We like the clinic at the Imperial Palace, which is open 8 a.m. to 5 p.m. seven days a week. The MGM also has an in-house medical clinic.

One caveat: you almost always have to pay up front for the services you receive. The clinics don't want to be bothered with the paperwork, so the onus of getting reimbursed by your insurance company falls on you.

Living Real Life

We find hundreds of things to do in and around Las Vegas outside of the gambling. First and foremost, we sightsee. We've gone to Hoover Dam, the Liberace Museum, the Imperial Palace Auto Collection, the magic museum at O'Shea's, even the Children's Discovery Museum. We've taken tours of the homes of the stars and the Thunderbirds precision flying team at Nellis Air Force Base. We like to tour factories and see how things are made. We've seen how marshmallows, potato chips, chocolate candy, cranberry juice, even clown figurines are manufactured—all within a 20-minute ride of the Strip. We take day trips out to Red Rock Canyon, Valley of Fire, and Lake Mead.

There are free bus trips that you can take to Laughlin, Mesquite, and Primm, all within a couple of hours of Las Vegas. You can gamble in all three places, but all have many non-gambling attractions and activities as well. Laughlin has the Colorado River running by, which hosts a number of water sports. Mesquite has lots of golf, mountain hiking, and a beautiful spa at Casablanca. Primm has golf and thrill rides. Since all of these places have hotels, they can be either day trips or overnighters.

We also take short trips to California. We like to go to the beach over Christmas, where the weather is usually a little warmer and there's a nice ocean breeze. We like to see the Christmas decorations on the yachts at Newport Beach.

A frequent activity for us is shopping. We prowl the Fashion Show Mall at center Strip and the two outlet malls at the south end of Las Vegas Boulevard. And if we want to do some window shopping, we walk around the Forum Shops and look at ridiculously high-priced luxury items—just as a form of entertainment!

We also spend time at the library, reading out-of-town newspapers and various magazines.

We've even gone to court (not because we've been arrested!). When you stay downtown, the county and city courts are right there within walking distance. Some of our most fascinating times in Las Vegas have been sitting and watching a good courtroom drama, particularly if it's a gambling case. You can always go in and ask the bailiff what interesting cases are being tried that day. He'll tell you what courtroom to go to. You go through the metal detector and sit in on any trial that interests you.

Another thing we do for recreation is bet on sporting events. We consider sports betting more of a non-gambling activity. Why? Because we bet on the game mainly for entertainment, since we're not skillful enough to make this an overall positive-expectation activity. We can sit in the sports book for a couple of hours and root for our money. Or if it's a Sunday morning during football season, there's nothing better than lying on our king-size bed, munching comped dinner leftovers, reading the Sunday paper, and keeping track of our parlay cards. This is a great entertainment value.

It's the same in the race book. When Brad gets tired of video poker, occasionally he'll go put a few dollars down and watch some horse races. Sure it's gambling, but it's more of a leisure-time activity than a hardcore run at a video poker machine or a blackjack table.

We don't neglect the spiritual part of life. Las Vegas has all kinds of churches, and we have Catholic friends who go to mass every weekend they're in Las Vegas. We volunteer, particularly at Christmas time, at the Salvation Army, just like we do back home, working on some of their programs for the homeless. One needs a balance between the body and the mind and the soul. And we like to keep that balance, even when we're in a casino town.

Postscript—Moving to Las Vegas

I originally wrote this chapter's conclusion in Indianapolis in 1997. After finishing the first edition of this book, I re-retired—or so I thought. I never dreamed that our life would change so dramatically and so quickly due to this book. The spectacular—and totally unexpected—success of *The Frugal Gambler* brought TV appearances, new writing projects, speaking engagements, and a ton of correspondence to answer from people all over the country who were embracing the frugal message. We un-retired, and we haven't stopped since.

It was an exciting life, but Brad and I quickly tired

of the flights back and forth to Las Vegas every time new publicity opportunities beckoned, and we were both weary of packing and unpacking as we moved every few days from one hotel-casino to another, even if it was all comped. So in 1999, we decided to buy a condo in this, our favorite vacation town, a place where we could escape the long dreary winters in Indiana. We could go back there every year when the spring flowers began to bloom and stay until the cold winds of late autumn would send us scurrying back to a more temperate winter.

We did that for one year, until we realized that we'd fallen out of love with the place where we'd spent most of our lives; we'd found a new love — Las Vegas. So when we went back to Indianapolis in spring 2001, it was to sell out and bid our final adieus to our Indiana home.

It's now 2005 as I write this postscript, and we've been busy and happy Vegas locals for four years. But this town is intense, and as much as we love the great life we have here, we sometimes need a break. So where do we go for a "thrill" vacation? Anywhere in the world where there isn't a casino!

10

Pyramid Power

In this chapter, I want to tell you about a few "real-life" gamblers I know. I've changed their names and some details to mask their identities. See if you can guess what level of the pyramid each is on.

These people are all very different, with individual low-roller agendas and routines. My hope is that by sharing some practical techniques of real-life low rollers (and one video poker professional), you'll see how it's done. Then you can pick and choose, constructing a low-roller program that best suits the priorities and preoccupations that are unique to you.

Sadie the Slot Lady

Sadie goes to Vegas three or four times a year and stays for three or four days at a time. When she first started visiting Vegas long before she knew us, she booked package deals through her travel agent that included her room and airfare. Booking a package deal is an economical and efficient way for first-timers, who don't belong to a slot club, to visit Vegas. It's usually cheaper to get a package deal through a travel agent than it is to make your own airline reservations and room reservations separately.

Back then, Sadie brought a bankroll of $3,000 or $4,000 with her. She'd start off on the dollar slots but when she lost too fast, she'd switch to quarters so her money lasted longer. Ultimately, she'd slow down even more by switching to $5-$15 bets at blackjack. She said she always lost playing blackjack too, only not as fast. She hadn't studied basic strategy; she was a typical hunch player. She'd gambled all her life and "kind of had a feel" for what she should do. She knew nothing about joining or using slot clubs. Sadie usually lost her whole bankroll, plus she paid cash for all her expenses.

After meeting us, her Las Vegas travel style changed dramatically. She still comes three or four times a year and stays for three or four days, she still has a bankroll of $3,000-$4,000, and she pretty much still loses it all. But now she stays in nice casinos, she is fully comped, and she sometimes gets her airfare reimbursed. She can also get a free room for her brother and sister-in-law whenever she wishes. She charges all of her meals to her room and never has to pay when she checks out. Just before she goes home, even if she's lost most of her bankroll, she gets hundreds of dollars of cash rebates from the slot club points she's earned. The casino picks her up at the airport in a limo and takes her back in a limo when she's ready to go home. (Sadie can't be bothered getting bumped off her plane; she just wants to get to Vegas as fast as she can, and when she leaves, she wants to get out of Vegas as fast as she can, lest she lose her rebate money.)

I've taught Sadie how to play video poker and she learned the simplified strategy for Deuces Wild. She's even hit a royal flush. You'd think this would help to keep her away from the slots. But she still loves to play them! She says, "I can play slots fourteen to sixteen hours a day. But after three or four hours of video poker, I'm too tired to remember what I'm supposed to be doing." This is a classic example of a player who feels that the expense is justified by the entertainment value.

Sadie is also a good example of how you can use some of the hints in this book even if you don't play a positive-expectation game. Because she feeds the slots, we can't help her win money, but we can and have helped her lose a little less, or at least go home with more money in her pocket than she otherwise would have. She now plays at the casinos that pay more to slot players than video poker players. And she no longer has to pay for her vacation.

Far be it for us to think any less of her. She's a senior citizen, she has a good retirement income and investments, and she can afford to lose what she does. She could easily visit any other vacation destination in the world and spend just as much money, but she doesn't like to do anything except gamble. She feels like she gets good value for her money. She loves being treated like a VIP.

Actually, Sadie could stay at one of the more upscale resorts in any casino destination. She might not get a limo to and from the airport, but she'd get the same cash rebate. All casinos like a slot player with a $3,000-$4,000 bankroll to blow. Caesars Palace, even the Mirage, will comp a room and meals to anyone who loses $1,000 a day. She could take this same money and do a lot more with it playing video poker or blackjack, because the house edge isn't anywhere near as high. But again, Sadie is simply someone who mostly wants to play the slots.

Hoosier Harry

Harry Winston is an elderly widower who lives by himself in a small apartment on a moderate fixed income from Social Security and a small pension. A veteran crapshooter, he likes to dress up every day in the style of an old-time gambler. He wears a starched shirt and suspenders, baggy pants with pleats, and spit-polished shoes, but he sports a casino cap instead of a thirties' Al Capone fedora, his nod to modern times.

He likes to take day trips to riverboats that are a two- to four-hour ride from his small hometown. He catches the casino bus early in the morning and gets home late the same evening. He pays $5-$6 for the bus ride, but he gets back a funbook with a free buffet and coupons for snacks and gambling bonuses, so his trip is basically free.

Because he's a regular at the Par-A-Dice in Peoria, the dealers and pit bosses have an affection for Harry. They know he's getting a little feeble and they'll pull up a stool so he can sit down and play for a while. And though he's not a big bettor, he's such a well-mannered old-timer that the bosses like to give him an extra food comp.

He's played craps ever since he was a boy. He likes to hang around the crap tables where the gambling is more sociable. He enjoys the camaraderie and he's not overly concerned about winning or losing.

Harry is a "tough" crap player; he makes $5 bets on the pass line and backs it up with $10 odds. He also places the six and eight. He knows that those are the best bets and he doesn't bother with the high-house-advantage propositions. If he's winning, he'll put a dollar on a hardway for the dealers. His main objective is to be with people. He has no interest in video poker (too solitary and his eyes aren't so good).

Three times a month he goes to the riverboat. He

divides his monthly bankroll into thirds and takes one third each trip. If it lasts the whole four hours, fine. If not, he goes to the snack bar and finds somebody to talk to, or goes to the top deck and enjoys the scenery as the boat cruises up and down the river, or nurses a beer at the pavillion bar and talks to his fellow losers while he's waiting for the bus.

Once in a while, after a big win, he might take a one-day junket to Mississippi, Tunica or Biloxi. If he gets really lucky, he'll take an overnight flight to Atlantic City.

Harry is a little like Sadie: someone who's devoted to a negative-expectation game, but stretches the value he receives in return for his inevitable losses. He's a conservative pass line bettor, so he faces the lowest house edge at the game, and by befriending the bosses he gets an extra comp or two along the way.

Frank and Linda Snowbird

Frank and Linda are retired. Back when they were still working, they went to Las Vegas occasionally, but spent most of their time in Atlantic City casinos, which was only a couple of hours from their home. However, once they retired, they had plenty of time; because they're video poker players, they wanted to spend as much of it as possible in video poker heaven. They still have a home in New York, but they spend the fall, winter, and spring at their condo in Vegas. As locals, they're not interested in room comps, but they occasionally need rooms for family and friends. (Almost all locals like to be able to get room comps when they need them, because when you live in Vegas, you get a lot of visitors. It's a fact of life for locals.)

The Snowbirds play at places that have good machines, good cash rebates, and good food comps. They gamble almost every day for two or three hours and eat a comped dinner in a casino. They diligently work the promotions.

Since they have both New York and Vegas addresses, they have the opportunity to get the most out of both kinds of slot clubs: those that cater to locals and those that cater to visitors.

Although they could afford higher stakes (they have a big bankroll), they stick primarily to the low-roller circuit. They don't play any higher than quarter video poker, because they don't like the tremendous swings that a steady dollar game brings. They play a very skilled game of video poker and only on positive machines. You will never see them at a slot machine. They're not out to make a living, they just want to have fun and they enjoy the challenge of beating the machines (they like to eat free, too).

Tim and Marla Busman

Our young friends Tim and Marla live in Las Vegas, work in the casinos, and have two toddlers. They came to Las Vegas in 1990 at the beginning of the big boom and got jobs at Excalibur just after it opened: he as a dealer and she in the marketing department. Since then, they've worked at a few other casinos and have a pretty good network of friends and co-workers who keep them up to date on the good promotions, slot club ins and outs, and general gambling opportunities.

When they first arrived in Las Vegas, they laid out a timetable for saving money until they accumulated a $5,000 gambling bankroll. Since both worked and expenses were kept to a minimum, they achieved their goal in eight months. While they were saving, Marla learned video poker strategy and Tim, being a dealer, studied card counting.

Now that they have two small children, they don't get to go out and play as often as they did in the beginning. Still, they manage to get out two nights a week, one night solo and the other together. On Marla's nights out, she plays quarter video poker and works the slot club circuit; Tim has a blast playing $5-$15 blackjack. They eat dinner out twice a week and never pay—his comps come from the pit bosses, hers from the slot clubs.

They take advantage of a few local promotions, such as paycheck cashing, football contests, triple-point days, and drawings. Last year Marla won an all-expense-paid week in London. They have an adequate bankroll, they gamble smart, they eat out for free, and they have a good life.

The Twins

Linda and Glenda are two high school math teachers. Linda is widowed, Glenda never married. They live together in Chicago, they're very thrifty, and they love to play positive video poker. They read all the gambling books and magazines. They go to Las Vegas for a week in the summer and several times over long weekends during the school year. Because they live in Chicago, a huge hub, they can take advantage of the many airfare specials to Las Vegas, and because they know far in advance exactly when they'll be flying, they can usually get the best advance-purchase bargains. Also, they fly during peak vacation periods, so they can sometimes get bumped. (Linda, who likes free airfare, always hopes to get bumped, while Glenda, who wants to spend as much time in Las Vegas as possible, hopes not to. Glenda, however, realizes how lucrative a bump is, and she makes Linda bet against getting bumped. That way if they do get bumped, at least Glenda wins the bet.) They can't take a bump coming home, since they're on a tight schedule for getting back to school.

The twins mostly play video poker, but they also play basic-strategy blackjack for a change of pace. In the early days of riverboats near Chicago, they investigated the video poker situation and found that the paybacks were too meager to bother with. But they paid attention to the changes that competition wrought over the years, and when they heard that the Empress at Joliet had installed positive-expectation Double Bonus poker, they programmed their video poker software and learned the difficult strategy. They can play Double Bonus with an expected return of a little over 100%; adding in the Empress' slot club cash rebate places them solidly in profit territory. They can now play winning video poker an hour's drive from their home. Plus they get lots of mailings from the Empress: coupons, two-for-one meals, invitations to parties, cash-back promotions, and the like.

The Empress allows Linda and Glenda to indulge in their favorite pastime between their trips to Las Vegas. Advantage players to the end, they're keeping an eye on the new Indiana riverboats about an hour's drive in the other direction and hope they soon will become more competitive by putting in better-paying machines.

Tex

Las Vegas is the only casino venue where a guy like Tex Harley could ply his trade. Like the Busmans, he also works in the casinos — not for, but against, them. In his early forties, still in the middle of his working career, Tex is a professional video poker player — he has no other job. He used to live in Texas, where he worked for years and saved a bankroll of $50,000, which he figured would be enough to see him through a worst-case six-month gambling dry spell. For three or four years up until the time he quit working, he'd go back and forth between San Antonio and Las Vegas, starting out with quarter video poker, then graduating to dollar machines. He already had a good relationship with several slot clubs, he knew all about the comp system, and he'd even had some contact with other video poker pros in town.

So he brought his $50,000 to Las Vegas, rented a small apartment, and started playing full time. Tex plays dollar and five-dollar machines. At those levels, he gets lots of comps and eats all of his meals in the casinos. He claims he hasn't been in a supermarket since he lived in Texas. Plus he can entertain his local and out-of-town friends lavishly. He makes a very good living, working an average of 10 hours a day.

More so than most, time is money for Tex, so he's very selective about the promotions he participates in. He concentrates on those that offer the highest dollar-per-hour return. Whenever there's an extra-special promotion going on, you'll find him hunkered down over a video poker machine or at a blackjack table—24, 36, 48 hours at a time. The only breaks he takes are the necessary ones: to eat, sleep, and run to the john. That's it. When a good promotion is happening, he has no friends, no pastimes, no life outside of the promotion. If the promotion has gone well, however, he can kick back and enjoy the fruits of his labors and renew his social life. (Is this the life for you? Probably not.)

It's a Jungle Out There

A word of caution here. I heard of another professional video poker player who came to Vegas with a

$100,000 bankroll. He started hitting positive $5 video poker machines and promotions hard. But despite his big advantage (often over 1% plus slot club points), after three months he was broke and had to return to his hometown. It's possible that he didn't play accurately or he used his bankroll for other expenses. This is a lesson for all of us: you won't necessarily achieve a particular percentage in any given length of time. Conventional wisdom holds that $100,000 would be enough for such a high-percentage-payback machine. But he suffered a very bad dry spell. It's possible that if he'd only had an extra $25,000 or so he would have hit enough jackpots to get even. It's also possible that if he'd had another $100,000 he still would've busted out.

Gambling is never a sure thing.

There are hundreds of examples of players trying to become professionals who eventually suffer the swings and arrows of outrageous fortune. More problematic are the thousands, if not tens of thousands, of Las Vegas locals who've gotten themselves into serious straights. Unless you have a sizable gambling bankroll that's completely separate from your living-expense account, you shouldn't be constantly haunting the casinos. Anyone can run into big trouble.

11

Ethics and Gambling
Odd Bedfellows

Think back to the story I told you in the Introduction about playing Uncle Wiggley, when my mother told me to spin for her and take her turn. I never once thought of giving myself an extra hop, or shorting her one. Being raised in a strict religious home, I knew from the time I was tiny that it was wrong to cheat. This ethic has never left me, as it did many of my friends. I know people who were raised the same way I was and they've had no problem cheating. Believe me, I've played with them and caught them at it. But I have a built-in standard against cheating of any kind. I could never cheat at a game for another reason: it would be no fun winning if I had to cheat to do it.

Some people may think this is an odd section to be in a book on gambling. However, you'll run into situations that require an ethical judgment time and time again in the casino, so you should be prepared to make the call.

The Casino as a War Zone

After I'd been gambling for a while, I realized that very little in a casino is black and white, ethically speaking. Going into a casino is kind of like entering a war zone. It's you against the house, and it starts to seem like the house has a license to steal. So if you get a chance to steal something back, you rationalize that it's only fair. When I started thinking that way, I knew I had to formulate a code of casino ethics. I'm not going to tell you what that entire code is, because it's a personal thing. You'll have to come up with your own code if you intend to "fight" in this battle zone.

My code is always being tested; I have to make ethical decisions in a casino all the time. Of course, some issues don't take any thought. If it's against the law, it's not even an option: for example, past-posting in blackjack (trying to increase your bet after you've seen your cards), or using an assumed name to avoid having to pay off your markers. But these no-brainers don't come up very often; the answer is rarely so cut and dried. So my personal standards are not static. In fact, writing this book has led to some changes in my behavior. There is nothing as sobering as opening up your actions to the bright light of public scrutiny. If I'm not willing to recommend a course of action in my book, then I'd better re-evaluate whether I should be doing it at all. The experiences in the sections below fall within my code. When you encounter these issues, you'll have to make your own decisions.

Coupons

If the casino gives you a funbook that has a 7-5 gambling coupon and specifies that the user is entitled to play "one coupon per person per day," it means you're only entitled to play that coupon that day. But what if you're with a few friends who give you their coupons to play? Does this mean that you can't use them all at the same time at different tables or in different pits? Does it mean that you can't use them all on the same day, but during different shifts? This is a gray area.

Some casinos restrict certain promotions to "one per visit." Talk about a gray area! What do they mean by a "visit"? A visit to southern Nevada? You have to go home and come back? A visit to Las Vegas? What if you take a day trip to Laughlin? A visit to the casino? What if you visit the casino in the morning and return that evening? We finally defined "visit" as follows. If I visit a casino in the morning and I come back again in the evening, I count that as two visits. If I have ten coupons that specify "one per visit," I feel that I can use one of them each time I walk into that casino. This is probably a light-gray area.

Back when I first started going to Vegas, I was such a coupon freak that I probably abused them. I didn't take "one per person per day" too seriously. I felt that it was one per person as often as I could get away with it. Different dealers, different pits, different shifts, whatever it took. Only if the casino took my name and put it in a computer did I respect the limits, because I knew then that I could easily get caught. I felt that since the casinos are allowed to do anything they can to suck you into all these games with their built-in casino advantages, using a coupon any time you could to grab a couple of dollars wasn't so bad. At least that's the way I rationalized it.

I don't want to sound like I've suddenly seen some kind of light, but nowadays I'm not so ravenous. I don't play coupons as much as I used to, so I often don't even use my one per person per day. Maybe I'm trying to make amends for when I used to go wild; maybe I'm letting it all even out now. Or maybe I've found that I can use my time better by participating in more profitable promotions. I'm not trying to imply that coupon freaks are unethical because they bend the rules whenever they can. It's a gray area, one that you'll have to deal with for yourself. And it usually involves such small dollar amounts that the casinos probably don't sweat it too much.

Tipping

A tip is a gratuity for services rendered, or for services that are about to be rendered. We all know that when you eat a meal in a restaurant in the U.S., it's standard to leave a tip that's equal to 15% of the bill. When a bellman delivers your bags to your room, when a valet brings your car from the parking lot, when a taxicab driver drops you off at the airport, you tip them. That's for services rendered.

You also tip in advance to get good service. You tip a showroom maitre d' in the hopes of having him take you to a better seat than you'd get if you didn't tip. Is that a tip or a bribe? There may be a fine line here, but no one thinks anything about it in a casino. When you arrive at a restaurant on a Saturday night and there's a waiting list, it's amazing how long it'll take to get a table if you don't tip the host or hostess, and how fast it goes if you do. If you pull up to the valet parking area on a Friday night and a sign says "Valet Full," it's miraculous how another parking spot appears, as if out of thin air, if you duke the attendant a ten.

Many casino promotions are handled by floor personnel and tipping will take you far fast. Whether it's a promotion that involves tickets for a drawing, stamps on a flyer, holes in a punchcard, or what have you, a well-placed dollar token in the hand of the issuer is an efficient way to earn more tickets or stamps or holes.

Once again, you have to use your own judgment to determine when a tip actually becomes a bribe.

Truth is, the whole casino comp system is ripe for abuse. Almost all casinos are set up to reward players for the amount of money they put at risk, not whether they win or lose. However, since many of the comps are distributed by fallible humans, it becomes a very subjective process. Many people will tell any made-up sad story about their losses in order to get sympathy from their slot hosts, which often leads to more comps. Table players will pocket chips; video poker players will pull their slot cards when dealt winning hands. I've heard of many people who have the most generous pit bosses and slot hosts on their Christmas gift lists. I'm not putting a judgment on any of this. I'm merely pointing out that everyone will have to draw his own line in the sand.

Malfunctioning Machines

This has rarely happened to me, but I've heard of many cases where video poker machines malfunction in the player's favor. Of course, this occurs infrequently, because the machines are well manufactured and the slot mechanics do good work. But one time a friend of mine landed on a video poker machine that was paying out more money than it should have.

Now, if I found a machine that malfunctioned in my favor, I would have to think long and hard about whether it was ethical to take the extra money.

One time on an Illinois riverboat Brad was playing a progressive video poker machine with the meter at $2,000 when he hit the royal. The progressive was supposed to reset to $1,000, but it didn't. For some reason the meter stayed at $2,000. The casino executives shut down Brad's machine after he hit the jackpot, fearing that if the same machine hit again, the meter might not reset for a second time. But they couldn't shut down the whole bank of progressive machines, because that would've upset a lot of people who'd been playing a long time trying to hit the progressive jackpot.

So the meter stayed at $2,000 and started climbing from there. Brad and I went to two other machines on the other side of the carousel and continued playing. Amazingly, less than an hour later I hit the progressive at $2,080! This is an example of a machine malfunctioning, but because the casino knew about it and allowed us to continue, it was no gray area for me.

Well, that second time the meter reset at $1,000, where it belonged, so we quit. And I don't mind telling you: those riverboat execs seemed awfully relieved to be rid of us!

Other People's Money

Sometimes you'll see a slot or video poker machine that already has credits on it and there's no one in sight. People leave machines with credits on them all the time. They're either drunk, disoriented, disgusted, or they simply don't know any better. Sometimes a machine runs out of coins while people are in the middle of cashing out and they don't want to stick around for ages to wait for a slot attendant to come and refill it, so they leave the remaining six or twelve or sixteen credits on the meter.

In most gambling venues, you can sit right down and play off those credits as if they were yours. In Illinois, on the other hand, all the riverboats have big signs in the casinos saying that you cannot take any money from a wagering machine or table that you did not put money into or onto for purposes of wagering (or something to that effect!). The fact is that in Illinois, even if you find money in the tray or on the floor, it's considered the casino's. To me, this is a little bit of a stretch. If I found money on the floor, it'd go into my pocket pretty fast and I'd defy anyone to tell me it wasn't mine. Here again, I feel that these places already have a license to steal, and now they want to steal the loose change off the floor!

One time I was in a casino in Las Vegas and I found this set of machines that malfunctioned by not accepting all the coins fed into it. It's not uncommon for a machine to miss accepting a coin here and there, which it shunts down to the coin return. Some coin returns are in non-obvious places, and with all the noise of the casino, players don't hear the coins drop out, then walk off without collecting them. This bank of machines kicked out more coins than normal, so by checking the coin returns and collecting the quarters, I walked off with quite a haul.

Well, the casinos have a name for this, I found out later. They call it "silver mining." They don't like it. One day a security guard spied my activity and said, "You can't do that." I told him that I found this money fair and square and no one was sitting at these machines. Then he told me that the unclaimed money belonged to the casino. Again, I don't buy it. I still look for coins in hoppers, but these days I'm a lot more subtle. At the time, I just said OK and left, but now I sit down, pretend I'm playing, and feel around in the coin return.

Queen of the Ziploc Bag

To take food out of a casino buffet or not—that is a burning question for me. For years I've carried Ziploc bags in my purse. They're good for all sorts of things. When I had little kids, I always had a wet washcloth in one to clean up dirty faces. These days I carry my slot cards in one Ziploc bag and I carry my coupons in another; you can see right through the bags and know which card or coupon to grab. You just never know what kind of situation you'll find yourself in where you'll need a Ziploc bag.

Well, buffets raise an interesting ethical question. Some buffets have signs that say, "Take all you want, but eat all you take." Well, what if your eyes are bigger than your stomach? Can you take the "leftovers" with you in a Ziploc bag you've brought in so as not to be "wasteful"? Does "eat all you take" mean eat it here, or can you take it with you and eat it later?

Of course, if the sign says, "Do not remove any food or drink from the dining room," it's pretty clear what the rule is. But what if there's no sign that says something to the effect that you're not allowed to remove food? Here's the gray area.

I've seen lots of people walk out of a buffet with an apple or orange in their hands. They make no attempt to hide it in a purse or a pocket or a daypack. It seems to me when casino buffets put whole fruit out, they're saying that it's all right to take this apple or orange with you.

What about if you've been comped to the buffet? When we're comped to a buffet, all I can say to the food and beverage managers is, "I would rather you not look in my purse when I leave." I might never have cheated at Uncle Wiggley, but you're apt to find a nice piece of ham or roast beef or turkey and a bun for a mid-afternoon or late-night snack, or strawberries to put on my cereal in my room the next morning. Maybe I rationalize a little bit here and think: well, I could go to the buffet in the morning on another comp and get a piece of ham and a bun, but I don't like getting up too early. I've got so many points in my slot club account at this casino that I could have three buffet comps every day for the rest of my life, so I'm actually doing the casino a favor by taking a little ham sandwich out of one buffet so I don't have to go down and do the whole buffet thing an extra time. You'll have to come up with your own answer to this dilemma, but they don't call me the Queen of the Ziploc Bag for nothing!

Taxes

The good old IRS! The reason that gambling and income tax is such a gray area is not only that you'll constantly be tempted to make an illegal move, but that you might not even know how to do the legal thing. How the IRS views gambling is a murky, swampy, stinky cesspool, so wide that it's extremely difficult to maneuver around. And at the same time the maps to help you get through it are inadequate.

Here are the basics. Technically, *any time* you win *anything*, you're supposed to declare it. This means that if you put a quarter into a slot machine on the way to the buffet and you get eight quarters back, you've won $1.75, and the IRS defines that as income. But it doesn't take a genius to realize that it simply isn't practical to try to keep track of every quarter you win in a casino. Even the IRS is sensible enough that it doesn't expect that sort of accounting.

Still, the IRS is savvy enough to recognize the potential for abuse in such a cash-crazy business, so it assumes that people will be lax in reporting their winnings. Accordingly, they've made some rules whereby the casino has to report how much you've won. The rules vary according to the game. If you play slot machines, video poker, or video keno and hit a jackpot of $1,200 or more, the casino gives you the dreaded W-2G, the form that documents your winnings. You now know that the IRS knows you've won. If you hit a jackpot of $1199.99, you're still required to report it to the tax authorities, but the casino is not. For some reason, the IRS is a little less stringent about live keno and bingo jackpots, which have to be $1,500 before a W-2G is issued.

You can write off your losses up to the amount of your winnings. This means that if you hit a $1,200 royal flush and can prove that you have at least $1,200 in gambling losses for the year, you don't owe the government any money. (However, if you lost $5,000 that year and won $1,200, you cannot deduct any loss for the amount over $1,200.) How do you prove it? Well, you have to keep records of your wins and losses. This is another ugly and murky swamp creature! I'll go into it in more detail below. For now, suffice it to say that if you can show you lost $1,200, then that will wipe out your win.

This doesn't mean you don't have to declare your win as income, especially since the casino files a W-2G on it. Also, to write off losses, you have to itemize your deductions (fill out a Schedule A). In other words, if you take the standard deduction and your gambling losses aren't enough to justify itemizing, then you have to pay taxes on the full amount of your winnings. Generally, one or two $1,200 jackpots won't make it worth your while to itemize if you don't in the first place. It's tax-paying time on gambling income for you.

My advice? If you don't itemize and you don't keep records of your gambling wins and losses and you happen to hit a jackpot of $1,200 or more, put 30% of it in an interest-bearing account and turn it over to the IRS the following April 15 (or make quarterly estimated tax payments if your winnings, plus other income, require it). That part's pretty black and white.

But if you play as much as we do and hit a lot of

jackpots, then you'll have to keep as accurate and detailed records as you can. To keep truly accurate records, you would have to list all your winnings and losses by the day (some even do it by the session), and it's entirely up to you how truthful to be, especially with regard to those winnings that aren't reported to the IRS by the casino. Here's the gray area, the ethical consideration. Will you underreport your winnings?

Some people don't keep records. They simply let the casinos do it for them. When you put your slot card into a card reader in a slot or video poker machine, the casino is not only reading it for points you're accumulating, it's also keeping track of how much money you're putting in and how much money you're cashing out. Most casinos will give you a print-out of those records at the end of the year.

That might sound convenient, but sometimes it isn't practical. Most casinos don't track your play year by year. In our case, for example, we'd been playing for several years before we started winning big and had to itemize our wins and losses. We didn't have many W-2Gs, so we didn't itemize and we didn't try to knock down our winnings by taking losses on Schedule A. Thus, we didn't have to ask the casinos for our slot club records.

Then one year we hit quite a few big jackpots and lost enough to make a difference against our winnings. We wanted to write off our losses, so we asked the casinos for our records. We thought they'd be broken down by the year, but they weren't. The records ran back to the day we first joined the slot club. The first year we wanted our records, we'd been members of the Stardust slot club for five years. All the Stardust gave us was a form saying that over those five years we'd put so many thousand dollars in and taken so many thousand out. We had to average out the wins and losses over five years, which the IRS may or may not consider acceptable record keeping. It usually wants personal records that corroborate the casino records.

So my suggestion is this. If you're going to gamble, you should start keeping a gambling diary. If you happen to get lucky and hit some big jackpots, you'll have a record of losses to subtract from the wins. A good way to keep a diary is to do it by the day, writing down your wins and losses, the casinos you played at, the games you played, the names of people you were with, what you ate in the restaurant (just kidding) — in short, every little detail that might matter if the time ever comes to "prove" to the IRS that your records are accurate and truthful. Some people are so detailed that every time they change machines they write down the machine's serial number and how much they put through.

These are just general hints. You really need to seek professional advice, preferably from a lawyer or accountant who's especially knowledgeable about the tax picture for gamblers.

If you keep a truthful diary of your wins and losses, then it's no longer a gray area. Only if you fudge the results of your gambling does it become an ethical question.

For full coverage of this vexing issue of taxes and gambling, you can buy *Tax Help for the Frugal Gambler*, an extensive special report written by Marissa Chien — a tax expert and a gambler herself — and me. See the Resources list for a description; it's available from Huntington Press for $25.

A Personal Postscript

After working on the various chapters of this book at different times, one night I read the first completed draft from beginning to end and I became slightly uneasy.

I'm keenly aware of the rapid spread of legal casinos over the past several years, and I've read and heard much discussion on whether or not this is a good thing. Are the economic benefits as positive as they are touted to be by the casinos? Is the number of addicted gamblers growing as fast as anti-casino advocates claim? Is gambling causing heartache in too many homes? I don't know the correct answer to these questions, but I do know that I don't want to encourage even one person to start out or continue on a path that will lead to negative factors in his or her life.

Gambling, although it plays an important part in our lives, is not an all-consuming passion. We have so many other interests — our families and friends, our volunteer work, travel, and education for self-improvement. Too much of anything is never good — and that's especially true of gambling. I want to stress the value of balance in one's life. I have touched on this subject in other places in this book, but I want to emphasize it again: Never let your gambling hurt yourself or anyone you love.

12

Breaking Even
is a Terrific Thing

Gambler's Prayer:
"Lord help me break even, for I need the money."

"So, how did you do?"

That was the most common question we were asked after we returned home from extended stays in Las Vegas before we moved here. Very often, we said that we broke even on the gambling and got all our expenses paid. People tended to turn up their noses and make some remark like, "What's the point of going?" They expected to hear a dramatic story that involved large sums of money changing hands. Breaking even is about as undramatic as it gets.

But here's how we figured it then, and figure it now. At the end of the year, we spent up to five months in casino towns. If we stayed free most nights, ate free once or twice a day, saw a few free shows, played up to eight hours a day, and recouped what we did spend out of pocket, we actually *made* money by breaking even. We didn't have to spend any of our own money, so our ordinary income continued to go into the bank and pile up. Anything we didn't spend was the same as winnings, and it was tax free to boot.

Look at it this way. If someone told you that you could take the kind of vacations that I've described in this book and you could do it all for free, would you also insist that you had to make some money while you were at it? Take home a profit from a free trip to paradise? Maybe, but that sounds a little greedy to us. If you spend half the year away from home with no expenses, it means that the other half of the year you have twice as much to spend at home. That was — and is — plenty "dramatic" for us.

This is the good life! And you can have it by playing quarter video poker and belonging to slot clubs and never being afraid to ask for what's coming to you. You can do it by being low rollers, just like we are.

Breaking even at gambling is a terrific thing, and we wish you luck in your quest to succeed at it.

Resources

Although this book gives you a solid foundation of information that can help you win more and lose less on your visits to a casino, many more resources will help you continue your studies to gamble smarter. There are too many to list them all, but the following are the ones I think you'll find the most helpful. These cover general topics and all casino games, especially video poker, which has an extensive resource list of its own.

Many of these resources are available in specialty gambling bookstores like the Gambler's Book Club in Las Vegas. Some can even be found in mainstream bookstores. For one-stop shopping, however, almost all of the products I recommend below can be purchased from Huntington Press, which has become the world's largest publisher of gambling books. Unless otherwise specified, contact Huntington Press, 3687 S. Procyon Ave., Las Vegas, NV 89103; 702/252-0655 or 800/244-2224 or go to www.GreatStuff4Gamblers.com.

As I've autographed thousands of copies of the first edition of *The Frugal Gambler*: The more you study the "luckier" you will be.

General Casino

More Frugal Gambling

My second book is your natural next step. It continues where *The Frugal Gambler* leaves off, 400 pages full of specific details on how to make your gambling bankroll stretch farther than you would ever have dreamed it could. I provide little-known details on how to score more slot club benefits, how to find and take advantage of more promotions, how to win more drawings, and ways to be a smarter coupon user. I delve into the complex world of comps to give you some of the secrets that have never been seen in print before. I have fat chapters on playing slots and video poker and a whole section on casino financial smarts, including a guide to tipping.

Comp City

This book, by Max Rubin, the funniest gambling writer I've ever read, is the one you must read if you play table games. Max shows you how to get $1 worth of comps for every 10¢-30¢ in casino losses. High and low rollers alike, at casinos anywhere in the country, can get lots of ammunition to use against the casino's assault on your wallet.

Las Vegas Advisor

If you visit Las Vegas even once a year, you'll want to become a member of the *Las Vegas Advisor*. It's by far the best source for keeping yourself up to date on everything Vegas: food, rooms, entertainment, gambling, and more. In addition, it gives you that "Vegas thrill" each month, even if you're snowbound in North Dakota in January, hundreds of miles from any casino. Anthony Curtis, publisher of the *LVA* and head of Huntington Press, is not only the most Vegas-savvy person alive today, he's a total nut for accuracy, so you can bet the farm on anything you see written or published by him. You also get complete access to the Web site at www.LasVegasAdvisor.com, including the member forums, the online newsletter, and the *Advisor* archive. Best of all, ordering the *LVA* is the most frugal thing you can do because you get back in coupons more than you paid for the subscription. The *Las Vegas Advisor* is available for $5 (single issue) or $50 (12 issues); an online option is available for $37 and includes the coupons (www.LasVegasAdvisor.com).

American Casino Guide

This venerable nationwide casino guidebook by Steve Bourie is updated every year and is an indispensable resource for traveling gamblers. It also has a good selection of gambling articles in the front of the book, covering many general casino topics and specific game information. My favorite section — of course! — is the one that contains coupons, $1,000 worth of them from casinos all over the U.S.

Steve's Web site, www.americancasinoguide. com, is also packed with useful information. There are more than 600 casinos described in his online list of U.S. casinos and links to the Web site of any U.S. resort-casino, riverboat, or Indian casino, all logically arrange by state. Another link takes you to a valuable list maintained by Scot Krause that gives current promotions going on in Las Vegas casinos. Want to know how much those slot machines you play returned in the past? Click the Slot Payback link for slot machine statistics in 34 different states.

Casino Player, Strictly Slots, and *Midwest Gaming and Travel*

These are three magazines that cover the gaming scene. I don't always agree with every single gambling concept that appears in these magazines, but overall, they can add useful knowledge for your casino visits. *Midwest's* Web site is www.midwestgamingandtravel. com, and www.casinocenter.com has links to both *Strictly Slots* and *Casino Player.* At both of these Web sites you can find selected articles from the hard-copy editions and subscription information.

Regional Gaming Publications

The following are good sources to find out about casino news and promotions in your area. I often have articles in: the New Mexico *Casino Entertainer* and *Jackpot*; the *Gulf Coast Entertainment and Casino News,* covering Mississippi coast and Louisiana casinos; and the *Southern California Gaming Guide,* which can also be read online at www.TheGamingGuide.com.

Michael Shackleford

Michael is definitely a math whiz; his nom de plume is the Wizard of Odds. His site, www.wizardof odds.com, is the first one I turn to when I have math questions about any casino game. It's loaded with gambling information on all the games, all of it based on sound math principles. Much of this information is now available in Shackleford's just-published book, *Gambling 102*. Also valuable is the long list (more than 200) of other gambling sites he recommends.

Web Sites

There are innumerable Web sites for the gambler who wants lots of information at his fingertips for various gambling venues. Here are some of the most helpful I've found:

Cuthbertson Media Group has the goal (and achieves it well) of bringing the casinos and players together with news, information, and reservations. Visit any one of these region-specific sites where there are lively forums led by the always cheery and enthusiastic guide, Jen Cuthbertson:

www.atlanticcityone.com
www.biloxione.com
www.casinos-one.com
www.lasvegas-one.com
www.tunica-ms.com

www.VPinsider.com is the home of Charles Lund's exhaustive online Las Vegas Slot Club and Promotions Guide, which tracks club details (such as cashback and point accrual), multiple-point promotions, sign-up bonuses, and paycheck-cashing bonuses. It's a comprehensive reference for any gambler who plays in a Las Vegas casino and wants to add as much value to his game as he can.

For very current casino news on the Vegas local scene, sometimes including juicy promotions, I read the *Las Vegas Review-Journal* daily newspaper. If you can't get the dirty-hands hard copy, you can read it online at www.reviewjournal.com.

Bilhere has an unbelievably long list of Vegas resources, including a comprehensive pool of coupons for buffets, shows, gaming guides, souvenirs, and more than 100 different activities for Las Vegas-bound travelers. Go to www.VegasResource.com, where you can also sign up for his packed-full-of-information e-mail newsletter.

Everything Las Vegas is a free twice-weekly e-mail newsletter to which you can subscribe at www.vegas lists.com/mailman/listinfo/everythinglasvegas. Its biggest asset is its numerous links to other Web sites where you can get the full stories of current happenings around town.

Tax Help for the Frugal Gambler

This is a special report I recently wrote with my financial advisor/tax specialist and fellow gambler/friend, Marissa Chien. We cover the subjects of what you should put in a gaming diary, what to do when you get a W-2G, and what tax filing options are available. We discuss the tangled tax web in which so many gamblers find themselves, and suggest guidelines that will help a gambler navigate the tax maze and avoid paying any more taxes than is required.

www.FrugalGambler.biz

At last I have my own home on the Web. Here you can find the details on all my frugal products, and it's the only place where you can order my books personally autographed. Also on this site is a calendar page, where you can find an up-to-date schedule of Brad's and my appearances on TV and in person, including book-signings and meet-and-greet sessions. On the homepage there is a link to my weekly column, Frugal Fridays.

Video Poker

An abundance of resources for the video poker player is on the market today. There's VP strategy software for your computer. There are books, strategy cards, and videos. But you must beware of "help" that's not mathematically sound. Just because you read something in a book doesn't make it true. It's only a cruel hoax when someone tries to sell you a VP system that flies against proven math principles.

To help you make wise decisions in buying VP products, here's a list of names of some gambling experts that you can trust to give you mathematically sound advice: Steve Bourie, Bill Burton, Jeffrey Compton, Anthony Curtis, Bob Dancer, John Grochowski, Skip Hughes, John (Lodestone) Kelly, Viktor Nacht, Dan Paymar, John Robison, Max Rubin, Michael Shackleford, Henry Tamburin, TomSki, and Dean Zamzow.

Following are my top recommendations for video poker resources. The first three "frugal" products are described in greater detail and can be ordered on my Web site: www.FrugalGambler.biz. Except where noted, all of these resources (and other choices) can be ordered from Huntington Press by calling 800/244-2224 or by logging on to GreatStuff4Gamblers.com.

More Frugal Gambling

After reading the VP chapter in this book, the logical place to continue your study is the sequel to this book. There, I present a more in-depth treatment of VP, giving 22 paytables to help you in your search for a good game. My daughter Angela, the Frugal Princess, who co-authored *More Frugal Gambling* with me, gives practical strategy hints for the beginning player, while I try to explain in simple language some of the more complex aspects, like dealing with volatility, sizing your bankroll, and playing multi-line games.

Frugal Video Poker **Software**

Although there are other software programs on the market, this newest one, developed by Jim Wolf, is the only one that combines the two elements you need to quickly and easily learn to play VP accurately. First, it's a no-money-at-risk tutor to guide you while you practice a game, pointing out errors that would cost you pain in your billfold at a casino. Second, it generates strategy charts that you can study while you're practicing, then print out and take into the casino with you for reference. This software has 54 pre-loaded games and the capability to adjust paytables to practice almost any new game that shows up in a casino. It has scores of other features for all players, from the beginner to the pro, including a tournament play mode, a way to figure the value of slot club benefits, and advanced math functions to analyze special situations.

Frugal Video Poker Strategy Cards

These color-coded laminated cards, developed by Skip Hughes, give a simplified strategy for many of the common VP games. Each strategy is easy enough for the beginning player to learn and suitable for the majority of gamblers to continue to use as they become more experienced. Most players will find that they can play much faster and more accurately and therefore achieve a higher return using these cards than trying to decipher the much longer and more complicated strategies. These cards were developed using the *Fru-*

gal Video Poker software. They're a necessity if you're learning VP without a software program.

Dan Paymar

This veteran VP writer has the following VP resources for the serious VP player: *Video Poker – Optimum Play*, a book of strategy help; *Video Poker Times*, a bi-monthly hard-copy newsletter; *All the Best of Video Poker Times*, a 100-page book including all of the best (and still useful) articles from the first 11 years of the newsletter; and Strategy Cue Cards for 18 casino VP games. See his Web site, www.OptimumPlay.com, for more details on these resources, ordering information, or joining his forum.

Bob Dancer

Dancer has put out a number of useful VP products, including a good set of strategy cards co-authored with Liam W. Daily. I especially recommend his and Liam's *Winner's Guides*, a series of books on individual VP games, if you want to pick one or two games in which you want to specialize and play with professional accuracy. I also recommend his autobiographical account of high-roller professional play in times now gone-by, *Million Dollar Video Poker*, an interesting read, with some promotion and slot club techniques that a low roller can still use today to increase the value of a VP play. You can read Bob's weekly VP articles at www.casinogaming.com/columnists/dancer.

Lenny Frome

The late Lenny Frome is considered the grandfather of expert video poker play and his son, Elliott, is following in his father's footsteps. You can find VP articles and product information at their Web site, www.vpheaven.com. *Winning Strategies for Video Poker* is a book that can be helpful to the player who does not have VP software, since it gives the strategies for 60 different games.

Web Sites

The following three Web sites give extremely valuable information so that the VP player can keep up-to-date in a rapidly changing casino world. I'm a member and contributor on the forums of the first two sites.

The site www.VPinsider.com, is maintained and moderated by Skip Hughes and Viktor Nacht and contains a valuable database chart, listing where all the best VP games are located at casinos all over the country. The site is loaded with other features, including the valuable Top 40 List, which gives detailed information about the best plays in any geographical region. There's a very lively forum where VP and other related topics are discussed. On the home page are links to other helpful sites and to information on subscribing to the Video Poker Player. This online magazine is packed with practical and specific VP information, presented in a hilarious style that makes it the ultimate laugh-and-learn gambling read.

The vpFREE Video Poker Group at http://groups. yahoo.com/group/vpFREE is a free Internet forum for the discussion of video poker and related topics. It has more than 3,000 members and is semi-moderated to provide a non-disruptive environment. Subgroups include an unmoderated free speech forum and thirteen regional forums. vpFREE also features a user-friendly video poker database that includes machine inventories and slot club and comp information on more than 275 casinos throughout the U.S. and Canada. Many valuable video poker resources and links can be accessed through the database. The vpFREE Video Poker Hall of Fame was established in 2002 to recognize and honor significant contributors to the growth and popularity of video poker. New honorees are elected each year by the members of vpFREE.

Finally, the site at http://videopoker.fws1.com is the work of the very busy VP scout "5-card" and is one that the serious VP player will consult frequently. There are pay schedules for more than 300 different VP games and their EV (expected value, or average return over the long term). His "Cost Per Hour" page shows you the price you pay for playing poor schedules, and the "Different Strategy" page shows what you'll lose by using a strategy that's not for that specific game. There's also a page with a long chart of data for progressive games and one with a good list of links that will lead you to more VP help.

Other Gambling Games

John Grochowski and Henry Tamburin have each written many practical gaming books, some with general casino information and many on specific casino games. Their books are based on sound math principles so you can always trust the information they give.

John has used a Q-and-A format for his Answer books on slot machines, video poker, craps, and video slot machines. He has the knack of translating often-difficult gambling math concepts into layman's terms.

Henry's Web site is http://smartgaming.com, where you'll find sound playing strategy tips for many casino games and a complete list of his books and videos. Although he writes about many casino subjects, his main love is blackjack, and on his Web site you can find a schedule of BJ classes he teaches and his recommendation of BJ resources. He also edits the *Blackjack Insider* e-newsletter, which is loaded with solid advice for blackjack players at all skill levels. This free newsletter contains reports of blackjack playing conditions in various gaming jurisdictions, strategy articles for novice players, card counting, and other advanced tips for experienced players, trip reports from pros, tournament strategy advice, tournament schedules, and product reviews. To subscribe, go to www.bjinsider.com, where you can also order the *Best of Blackjack Insider* e-book, which contains a collection of 40 articles from previous issues of the newsletter (including mine on blackjack and comps).

Knock-Out Blackjack and *Burning the Tables in Las Vegas* are among the best blackjack books available today.

Ken Smith, a highly respected blackjack expert, has two extremely helpful Web sites for BJ players: www.blackjackinfo.com and www.blackjacktournaments.com.

BlackjackInfo.com provides complete information about casino blackjack, starting with a complete explanation of the rules. The main draw of the site, however, is the Blackjack Basic Strategy Engine. You can plug in a particular set of rules for blackjack for a casino you plan to visit, and the Engine will produce a free basic strategy chart that's customized for that exact game. There are plenty of places where you can find a blackjack basic strategy chart, but BlackjackInfo makes sure that you get the best possible chart for your situation.

BlackjackTournaments.com covers the new hot branch of blackjack tournaments. Recent broadcasts of the "World Series of Blackjack" and the finals of the Las Vegas Hilton's Million Dollar Blackjack tournament have generated a surge of new interest in the game. Blackjack tournaments often provide great value for a smart gambler, with free or discounted rooms and meals, and of course a chance at big prize money. But BJ tournament strategy is much different than what you use when you are playing in a regular casino game. BlackjackTournaments.com discusses these new strategy points and provides an online community for tournament players, where they can share information.

Viktor Nacht's AdvantagePlayer.com, presented by RGE Publishing, Ltd., features extensive resources for the video poker, slot machine, blackjack, and roulette player. The blackjack channel is the home of blackjack author and teacher Don Schlesinger, featuring his subscription area, Don's Domain and the Masters of Blackjack, where he and a half-dozen of his peers share sage advice and produce groundbreaking new research on the latest blackjack techniques. There are also free blackjack forums, the busiest of their kind, where many of the top players in the world contribute. From this site there is a link to Trackjack.com — a database-driven, information-sharing BJ network that tracks table conditions (variations in rules and procedures), user comments, and news items. It's organized by casino and accessible through simple regional navigation or various custom-built search engines. You can import table conditions from Trackjack directly into the Casino Verite blackjack training program and the CVCX betting optimizer.

Too many books on slot machines contain, at best, half-truths or, at the worst level, downright false information that the math cannot support. Along with John Grochowski, whom I mentioned earlier, John

Robison, author of the *Slot Expert's Guide*, is one of the few writers about slots that give helpful information that will pass the good-math test. Even though slots are almost never beatable, this book provides valuable information on how to play them at the lowest cost. John's website is www.slotexpert.com.

Poker fever is sweeping the country these days, thank to the many televised tournaments. There are a multitude of poker books out there; some of the best are written by Mason Malmuth and David Sklanksy. I especially recommend *Get the Edge at Low-Limit Texas Hold 'Em*, by Bill Burton, if you want a good beginner's book to help you jump into this popular form of poker. His book is the most basic and simplistic book on Texas hold 'em to date. Bill's journey from the kitchen table to the casino poker room is every poker player's dream. It's available at www.billburton.com. Bill Burton is also the Casino Gambling Guide at www.casinogambling. about.com, where he writes a weekly column covering topics about all aspects of casino gambling. His motto is "Luck comes and goes. Knowledge stays forever!"

Index

About the Author

Since the publication of best-selling *The Frugal Gambler* (which reached second in sales on Amazon.com—behind Harry Potter), author Jean Scott has become a household name to millions of low-rolling casino visitors. She is in continuous media demand and has been featured on "Date-line," "Hard Copy," "To Tell the Truth," numerous Travel and Discovery channel documentaries, and "48 Hours." She and her husband Brad live in Las Vegas.

**Meet the rest of the Frugal Nation and tap into
the best Las Vegas information on the Web.**

www.LasVegasAdvisor.com

Free features include:

• **Frugal Fridays:** The Queen of Comps'
own weekly report on the Las Vegas bargain scene.

• **Las Vegas' Top Ten Values**

• **Freebies & Funbooks:** An updated list of
the best casino coupons and promotions to
stretch your vacation budget.

• **Vacation Planner:** A complete listing of headline entertainers, production
shows, special events, gambling tournaments, weather reports, transportation
info, and area maps.

Member features include:

• **Members Only Section:** Check out current and back issues of the *Las Vegas
Advisor.*

• **Discounts:** Members receive special pricing on all Huntington Press products.

• **Exclusive *LVA* Forums:** Talk with the Queen of Comps, other gambling
experts, and your fellow Vegas aficionados.

Log on now!

Frugal Video Poker Software

Frugal Video Poker (*FVP*) is the latest and greatest in playing/tutoring/analysis software for video
poker players. This program is the first to bring
together the two vital features of analysis and play-
strategy generation. *FVP* includes many valuable add-
ons not available in other programs, such as the ability to incorporate slot
club returns into overall payback calculations. With 54 pre-loaded games,
including most popular variations of Jacks or Better, Bonus (Double,
Double Double, Triple, etc.), Deuces and Joker Wild, as well as the ability
to customize the paytables to represent virtually any game you'll find in
a casino—*FVP* offers video poker students an extensive range of game
options. The CD comes with an 11-minute video in which Jean Scott appears to explain the fundamentals of video poker play.

*System requirements: Windows 95 or higher, Pentium 100 Mhz or faster, 8 MB RAM,
SVGA monitor, CD-Rom, mouse, Windows-compatible sound card.*

4/13 ②　11/11
4/17 ⑤ 9/16